THE STRUGGLE TO SUCCESS

HOW I TURNED LIFE LESSONS INTO PROFITABLE BUSINESSES

WILLIAM HEGMANN

with DUNBAR CAMPBELL

Bookmark
PUBLISHING HOUSE

This is a work of creative non-fiction. The author has made every effort to share true and accurate recollections. Some events, conversations, and situations have been dramatized. While all the stories in this book are true, some names and identifying details have been changed to protect the privacy of the people involved.

TABLE OF CONTENTS

INTRODUCTION

I was never supposed to make it. At least, I never thought I would live past twenty. The people I knew while growing up will tell you the same thing. No one is supposed to live with the dangers, fear, and pain that were a daily part of my life growing up in Galveston.

But I survived it, which is why I want to tell you about it in this book. It's not just about survival but how I turned the lessons I learned on the streets to build a successful business and a plentiful lifestyle for my family.

For those who crossed me or those I might have crossed, let bygones be bygones. At our age today, we can now shake our heads in disbelief that we came this far with the odds against us. Maybe we survived for a reason. All of us Galveston boys should now agree that no one should experience what we went through, especially as teenagers. We are now the grown-ups we wished we had around us with sons and daughters to show the light. Let's turn this experience into lessons for them, so they will never know the struggles we faced.

True, we may move on, but the memories will still live. Every day, I pinch myself to see if my escape from the angry disadvantaged neighborhoods of Galveston was just a dream. Sometimes I return there and walk those streets again, so I never forget how far I have come.

Never in my youth did I dream about having the life I have today. Maybe if I did, it was just to mentally escape my reality until the echoes of gunshots jolted me from my fantasy. Today, that crazy dream has become my reality. I tell you that not to say, "Look what I have accomplished," but to say, "Look what YOU can accomplish."

Am I proud of everything I did? Absolutely not!

I was handed a rotten deck of cards from the beginning. But I played the hand I was dealt in my youth. It was all I had. Broken home. Dropout in ninth grade. Dangerous streets. To survive in the moment, I often did things I would later regret. I hurt others. Others hurt me. I took from others. Others took from me.

I didn't make the rules; I just lived it every day. That's just how things were.

It was all I knew—except for the shelter my paternal grandmother, Nanny, provided. During my childhood turmoil, she was my savior.

My parents split up when I was only an infant. Sounds familiar, right? My father continued to live with Nanny, while my mother, of Hispanic heritage, moved ten city blocks away. I spent my youth alternating between those two homes, but the difference between the two was the difference between heaven and hell.

Now, don't get me wrong. I am not bitching because I am some spoiled brat accustomed to getting everything he always wanted. My luxuries included bicycles built from parts I salvaged from old, abandoned bikes lying around alleyways and street sides. My games were cheap-ass Nintendo games from Walmart that my father bought me once in a while whenever he had a few dollars to spare. I was not even blessed to have quality time with my parents. As a kid, the most valuable thing I had was time with my grandmother, Nanny.

Born to German parents, Nanny was the closest I ever came to meeting a real saint. She nourished the humane part of me, which I needed to have hope in my future. Even today, I can still smell the aroma of her fried pork chops and macaroni floating through the screened door as I ran up the front steps to her verandah.

I treasure the memories of Nanny and her warm home. After she passed away, I returned to Galveston and bought the house she had rented for 30 years. She always wanted to buy it, but life never afforded her that opportunity. So, I did it for her! It means more to me than just wood, walls, and glass. Nanny and her house saved my life.

To understand my life, you also must understand Galveston, Texas. Most people might know it as a coastal city of 60,000 people, three miles wide at its widest point and thirty-two miles long, where tourists flock to have fun on sunny beaches. But when I was growing up, there were two Galvestons. One Galveston attracted visitors to have fun on the coast, and the other Galveston imprisoned residents in vicious cycles of crime, poverty, and despair.

While tourists found pleasure in places like Moody Gardens and Flagship Hotel, I still recall places like Cedar Terrace and Park Land with fear. These were government-designed and managed projects, breeding grounds for more than twenty gangs, like the Bloods and the Crips.

The people from my Galveston did not meet in fancy restaurants like Gaidos to dine and negotiate business deals. They met in open streets like Winnie and 39th, Tenth and L, and 55th at M to deal drugs and trade gunfire.

That reality surrounded me every day. Winners gained money—lots of it. Losers gave blood—lots of it. Those were my choices. Constantly.

I was a young Hispanic-looking boy, with a German name, in a neighborhood that was eighty-percent black. I was a minority within a minority, in a community at war with itself. To go from Nanny's house to my mother's house and back, I had to cross forbidden lines between Bloods and Crips territories. Death could come just for wearing the wrong color clothes.

Each time I crossed Broadway Street, it was a hard transition back to my mom's. That neighborhood was listed as one of the most dangerous neighborhoods in Texas and the entire country. I didn't know the crime statistics back then; all I knew was the fear. But my scar reminds me today that I was included in those numbers.

Those who knew me then are surprised I made it past twenty.

When I visit my old neighborhoods now, the sounds and smells of the humid city still greet me. The trains still rumble by, and the breeze still rustles through palm trees to deliver the scent of seaweed. The broken bicycles I used to scavenge to build my own lay abandoned and lonely in dark alleyways, among discarded beer cans, broken bottles, and strung-out drug addicts.

But most of all, the memories of the people—the few I cared for and the many I distrusted—still trouble me.

Occasionally, I run into people I used to hang with—those still alive and not in prison. We all know other friends and enemies, too numerous to count, whose last farewells were front-page headlines, young lives cut short by drugs or bullets. If we talk, our conversations are frequently broken by long moments of silence, in solemn respect for what once was. Sometimes we laugh to soothe the memories—in amazement that we are still here, alive. But we still look over our shoulders—just in case.

Although, when I see old acquaintances from my drug-dealing days, we don't shake hands. We nod at each other with cautious glances. Sometimes, we avoid eye contact or just avoid each other altogether. If we talk, we do so hesitantly and move on. People died for saying the wrong thing at the wrong time. A misunderstood word or a look of disrespect was the last thing many said or did seconds before their lives ended.

Old habits die hard.

Almost everyone I knew, family or acquaintances, had hidden motives that left physical and emotional scars on me or others. Few helped build positive memories in my youth. While Nanny was my lighthouse, my beacon of light during the darkest days of my life, others were like deceitful rocks on the shoreline, waiting and plotting to sink my ship.

Or even to take my life.

Those stories come later in the book. For now, I can admit that both the good and the bad molded me into who I am today. But I had to choose to separate my future from my past—like a drunk waking up from a bad hangover and saying never again—and meaning it.

I am ready to tell as much as possible to help others see a way out of their hell. But to do so, I will protect the guilty and shelter the innocent. This book isn't meant to cause harm; it should help those who need to know there is a way out.

This book is not about getting even with the past so that others may learn to avoid what I went through. That's it. Period. I want to keep it real, so my language might not be the cleanest at times. It's not meant to offend; it's just the reality I lived. No one will get hurt from these pages. There's been too much pain already. Pain was my teacher, and I want to pass the lessons I learned to anyone who wants to listen.

I want to be a teacher for change without others getting hurt.

This is time to reflect on the harsh lessons my life taught me and pass them along to a new generation, so they don't repeat my mistakes. To teach that their future is not a mirror of their past.

If this book teaches you one thing, it's this:

If I can rebound from the past I lived, anyone can.

That's my message. Take it or leave it.

Don't let my tattoos, rugged good looks (my wife agrees!), and street talk fool you. Deep inside, I am just like everyone else. I want success and happiness, not just for me but also for my family and friends. That's what you want, too. If that's why you're reading this book, I won't disappoint you. I won't hold any punches. I'll spare you no detail, except when I do so in respect of, or to protect, others.

I'll tell you about the struggles in my own words, but I won't leave you hanging there. I'll show you a way to success that worked for me and many others. This book is about struggle. It is about success. It is about my life, my *struggle to success*.

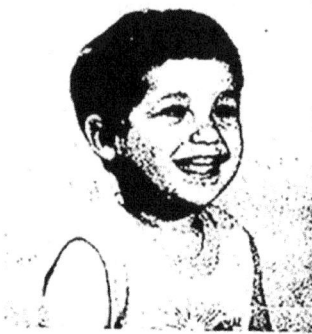

William Frederick Hegmann IV,
son of Linda and Bill Hegmann,
was 2 years old Thursday. He has
three sisters, Linda, Lilia and
Krista; grandparents are Mr. and
Mrs. Manuel Martinez Sr. and
Mary Christine Hegmann.

For my second birthday, my dad (with me below) posted the above picture
in the Galveston Daily Newspaper, August 25, 1986. He used to deliver that
newspaper.

CHAPTER ONE

LIFE WITH MY FATHER

The best place for me to start my story is at the beginning. I was born William Frederick Hegmann IV on August 21, 1984, in Galveston, Texas. That was the year Ronald Reagan won a second term as president, crack cocaine was first introduced in Los Angeles, The Terminator movie with Arnold Schwarzenegger came out, and Prince released his hit song, "When Doves Cry."

To my knowledge, only one of these events directly impacted my life.

Why do I tell you this? Because I want to clearly state my beliefs from the beginning. Significant political or star-studded Hollywood events don't impact your life like the real shit that comes your way every day. That's why it's called reality.

My reality sucked, but it made me who I am today. I was born into a reality that made all that other shit on TV look like Mickey Mouse games, but they gave me valuable lessons I still live by.

My father, the third William Hegmann in his German lineage, was a real hero to me in my youth, or so I thought. I loved and respected him. As young boys do in their innocent years, I looked up to my father. He did a lot with me and for me. Some I never knew until years later. For example, in 1986, the Galveston Daily News ran an announcement of my second birthday with my full name, William Frederick Hegmann IV.

My dad did lots of odd jobs back then, including newspaper delivery. Now I wonder if he had asked them to print it, so I would one day say he had a heart. But this was long before I discovered he had sinister demons that turned him into a monster.

My dad could be traced back to my great-great-grandfather, Dietrich Hegmann, who was born in Germany in 1844 and moved to Galveston in his youth. He became captain of the schooner, "Lady Dora," and started the tradition of naming the first-born son William. His son (my great-grandfather) was the first William, followed by my grandfather, then my father, and now me.

Dietrich also had another son, Otto Hegmann, who drowned at age twenty off his father's schooner in Galveston's San Luis Pass in 1896. Despite diligent searches, his body was not found for two days. It was not until a Lyle gun was used to blast gunpowder charges at the scene that the body rose to the surface.

It seemed my great-great-grandfather had started three traditions that would catch up to me one hundred years later: the name William, pain, and gun blasts.

My great-grandfather was a member of the Karankawa Tribe Number 15 Order of the Redmen. At first, I was excited to claim some proud Native American heritage until I discovered that membership in the Order of the Redmen was only for white men. So, I have a family tree with names like Otto and Dietrich on my father's side. Go figure. The people I grew up around would laugh their asses off if they knew this! Most of them still think of me as Mexican.

My Hispanic blood comes from my mother, Linda Hegmann, who was a Martinez before marrying my father. From her lineage, I am related to people with names like Manuel and Esequio. When she married my father, he moved his bride, a special education teacher, into my grandmother's house on 2918 Ave O1/2. Honestly, I am not 100% positive about some of the history here, so I am sometimes guessing. That's how little I know of my parents' past.

Before I was born, my mom had given birth to my three sisters, Lilia, Linda, and Krista. For reasons you will soon learn, I wish I had been born years before them. They needed an older brother to protect them. It would be years later before I knew that they also held dreaded memories of a different kind. I love them. I respect them. I admire them for their bravery and strength. Some of their experiences are still sensitive, but with their permission, some of their stories will briefly show up in this book.

But back to Dad. My earliest memories of him are of his generosity and the times he spent with me, like going shopping.

"Son, you want to go to Walmart with me?" he would ask.

I didn't need much persuasion. "Yeah!"

He would carry me on his shoulders around Walmart, buying me Nintendo and Sega games and stuff for my bike—reflectors, bells, and spray paint. I can picture him in his regular pearl snap button-downs, jeans, and cowboy boots. That's all he ever wore. And, of course, his big-ass belt buckle!

He smoked cigarettes, did crossword puzzles, and loved Country music. He didn't drink much, but he loved food. Give him the kitchen, and he'd always cook chicken or pork chops. But when he wasn't cooking, his favorite food at home was Nanny's hamburger impossible pie. I could taste it now. It was a labor of love for her. I could see her mixing ground beef, cheese, eggs, and bisques. And when the oven filled the house with the aroma? Lookout. Both Dad and I would chomp into our first slice like hungry lions having their first meal in weeks.

I believe Nanny enjoyed cooking for us because it gave her pleasure to see her son and grandson together, eating, joking, and laughing like a family should—like the family she felt slipping away from her for dark reasons only she might have known at the time. As a kid, I was too oblivious to see that. Looking back at those times, they taught me one thing. When people love doing something, the reason for doing it could be something more than the act. Nanny's cooking was the act. Having a happy family around was the reward she wanted desperately but could never quite get. Maybe that's why she had such sadness behind her big-rimmed glasses and soft smile.

I have no doubt my dad was one of Nanny's disappointments. As a kid, I thought he was the smartest man because he loved reading. Yet, he never seemed to find that spark to do more with his life. All his attempts in business failed. I guarantee you that if he knew he would end up in Chapter One of my book, reaching as many people as it will, he might have lived his life differently. Maybe. Or maybe he might have hidden his dark side better—like he did his drug habit.

His anger was rare at first. He only displayed irritation when someone disagreed with him or told him no, or if he didn't get his way. That might be the reason he couldn't stay married to my mom. I don't remember them exchanging a word between them in kindness or anger. But I felt the tension; it was so thick you could slice through it with a Samurai sword. By the time I came along, whatever drove them to say "I do" on the alter had vanished in a Galveston sunset. Never to return.

If my father had any friends before I was born, I never met them. As I was growing up, he had only a handful of acquaintances and one very close friend I can remember. Patricia Remington. We all called her Patty. Patty and my dad spent many hours talking and laughing, and I guess that's what made them friends. He always seemed happy around her.

I was always happy around him too, and maybe that's why I don't remember him ever getting angry at me or spanking me. My times with him were for father and son to bond, and we did, at least in the early years. When he was not driving his taxi or delivering newspapers, he would nod at me with a cigarette dangling from his lips.

"Let's go for a ride, son."

He never had to ask me twice. I would rush to get my bicycle and follow him with his into the front yard.

Nanny, ever watchful over me, her only grandson, would stare at him with concern. "Bill, where are you taking him?"

"Same place as always, Mom. Dutch Kettle."

"Better get him back here safe."

He would blow his cigarette smoke in the breeze. "As always, Mom."

"I'll be watching the clock. Be careful out there with him."

Nanny cared. Really cared. It showed in those moments. She and my sisters were the only adults who showed me love as a child.

Dad and I would wave goodbye to her as we rode down 29th Street toward the sea, where we would cross the busy Seawall Boulevard to the ocean side. The steady breeze against my face would blend with the salty-seaweed aroma, the sound of the waves, and seagulls overhead—a moment of perfection with my dad.

I had memorable moments with my dad that every boy my age would also cherish with their dads.

My dad and I would ride our bicycles a few minutes along the seawall; then, we would cross the street again to the Dutch Kettle at 3618 Seawall Boulevard. There we would look for a window seat. We would talk and laugh, point at passing cars and people, and gaze at the horizon as we gobbled down steaming scrambled eggs and grits. I still hold on to those memories to this day.

It amazes me how the best memories with my dad were all about us doing simple shit like that together. He never took me to Disney Land or Sea World. He never took me on a plane or a train. He never bought me a car, like most teenagers today expect from their parents. Hell, he never even bought me a new bicycle. My bicycles were mismatched parts from salvaged beat-up bicycles I found around the neighborhood. I had to spray-paint them to make them look halfway decent. My father couldn't afford to pay for a roof over his head. I didn't care that he couldn't afford to buy me a bunch of expensive shit. I enjoyed playing the video games he bought me. But that was not the most important thing I remember about my early years with my dad.

What I most wanted from my dad is what every kid wants from a parent—their time and attention.

Today, I still take that lesson seriously with my girls. I spend as much time with them as I can find with my busy schedule, and sometimes I even get lost myself. We are usually hanging out at the house watching TV or playing games. We drive everywhere together, even if just going to pick up some fast food. It is more valuable to kids than all the games, bicycles, and skateboards you could buy.

Back in Galveston, I expected that life with my father would forever be made up of happy moments together. I had no idea how wrong I was.

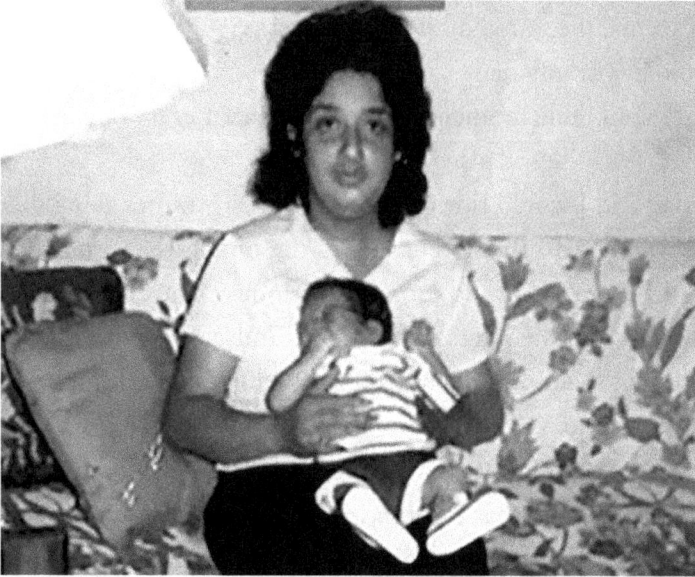

My mother with me (above) and with Roland (below).

CHAPTER TWO

LIFE WITH MY MOTHER

I believe there was a time when my mom was as loving and compassionate to me as Nanny. But as hard as I try, I can't recall a minute of it. As an adult, I wonder if it was because she never had it to give. How she managed to become a special education teacher caring for children is still puzzling to me. I sometimes like to think that maybe she gave so much of her heart and soul to her special-needs students that there was none left for her three daughters and one son.

It wasn't that she gave nothing from her heart to her children. If that were the case, hell, that would have been awesome! Zero would have been frigging fantastic over what she gave us. Instead, she taught us how to distrust, especially friends and family. To this day, I don't use the terms *friends* and *family* lightly. My mother had an amazing ability to turn her kids against each other. Even after she passed away, I am still mending the divisions she sowed between my sisters and me. It is sad to say, but to this day, my favorite description of her is *The Master Manipulator*.

Her attention was always pulled in directions other than toward her family. That could be why my father started looking elsewhere, but I don't know their whole story. My father was no angel either. They were not good for each other or their children.

Probably the best way to see the value my mother placed on her children was when she decided to move us after her breakup with my dad. My dad moved in with Nanny, and my mom moved with us kids to 3907 Avenue H (Ball Street), between the dreaded Broadway Avenue to the south and Blood territory Parkland (Palm Terrace and Sand Piper Cove) to the north. During my years there, it was one of the most dangerous neighborhoods in America.

I didn't know statistics then, but to any adult who cared, the headlines told the story. Galveston's crime rate was fifty percent higher than the national average. Murders, robberies, and assaults occurred daily, all around us, especially in my neighborhood. I don't know why my mother, or any mother, would consider raising children in that environment. I don't want to make excuses for her, but maybe like other desperate single mothers, she wanted to leave and had no choice. That I could understand. So why did I never hear her talk about wanting to leave? Through her choices, she made it clear that the safety of her children was not her priority.

That experience gave me the motivation to make better decisions for my children. I work hard to provide them with a safe, happy environment so when they are adults, they can look back at their early years with fond memories.

Even if my mom had it in her to love and protect her children, she wasted most of her time obsessing over her boyfriend—and money. Both of which she failed to manage well.

My mom's boyfriend, Roland, was a retired soldier, and he was older than her. He kept to himself most of the time and never seemed available for a friendly conversation like I enjoyed with my father. The more distant Roland became, the harder my mom tried to win his attention. And she threw everything she had into that project. He drained from my mother the last ounce of affection she might otherwise have had for her children. She spent all of her energy and money on him.

In my mind, as teenagers longing for the presence of a mother in our lives, she gave Roland all the attention we all needed from her. He knew it. I knew it. He didn't like me. I didn't like him. We both worked really hard to keep it that way, and my mother didn't care.

I remember a conversation she and I had one day as she was getting ready to visit Roland.

"Go change your clothes," she said in her typical demanding tone. "We're going by Roland's."

"I don't want to go see him."

"I don't care if you like him or not," she yelled. "We're going, and that's that!"

"He never even talks to me."

"So what!" she shouted. "At least he treats me better than your miserable father."

At that time, I still liked my father and was tired of her daily insults about him. I stomped off to change my clothes. None of our conversations ended well.

In all fairness, Roland did have one good thing: access to a swimming pool in his apartment complex. So, during our visits, my sisters and I swam in the pool while our mom stayed in the apartment with Roland.

As bad as it sounds, my mom's craving for money gave me a glimmer of hope that she and I could have a relationship. I learned early that money increased my value to her, but only so long as I had some to give her. And it didn't matter what I did to earn it. Even after she learned that my cash flow came from illegal drug sales that could have landed me in jail for a long time, she encouraged it and participated in it. She made time for me as long as I provided her with money. I'll go into more details later.

One good thing, or maybe bad thing, she did for me at age fourteen was help me get my driver's license. My mother had a heart condition that required another driver in the house, and my sisters were no longer living there. By law, when I turned fourteen, I was permitted to have a hardship driver's license. I often wondered why none of my three sisters stayed longer, considering our mom's heart condition. The answers to those questions did not come until years later.

My driver's license picture showed me in a t-shirt, chain, and the first evidence that I could grow a mustache one day. Just as quickly as I began to learn the streets by foot and bicycle, I started learning the streets from behind the wheel of a car. By age fifteen, I knew every street corner, gang territory, gambling shack, and dope house in Galveston. With that knowledge, I began to earn quick money as a supplier—a lifestyle that exposed me to unknown temptations and dangers.

I still have more questions than answers today. I was being raised by broken parents with shattered dreams in a violent city. By the time I was old enough to figure out that my life was not normal, I was too busy surviving on the streets to ask why.

But reasons didn't matter.

What mattered was learning the rules, not the laws, because those never protected me on the streets. To me, laws were strange games practiced by weird motherfuckers in suits surrounded by stacks of books. And they sent out their goons in blue uniforms, driving slowly up and down the streets with spotlights on just to harass us. That was the law. The more distance between us and the law, the better. If they approached us on the streets, even to talk, we ran. Anyone who walked was considered a bitch. So, I ran too. I ran a lot in Galveston.

Street rules were not written in books like laws are. The rules were permanently scorched into my brain by fear, pain, and excitement. Yes, there was something exciting about living on the edge. I learned and practiced those rules when my mom moved us to crime-infested Ball Street.

I was probably younger than ten when I witnessed how powerful and unforgiving street rules were, compared to weak or nonexistent laws. One day, I was sitting alone on my mom's porch facing our street. It was quiet, just after sunset on a warm evening, the heat soothed by a steady breeze that blew in from the gulf. A train clanked past a few blocks behind us, along Harborside Drive. To my right, two bicycles rode down the street toward our house. Not unusual.

But as the two bicycles drew closer in the gray night, I became concerned. These two young men were wearing shades of blue, the colors for the Crips. I lived in Blood territory. As far as I knew, it was not in any law book, but it was a street rule that Crips stay in Crips' territory and Bloods stay in Bloods' territory. Or risk being killed.

As the men rode slowly past our house, a car rolled down the street behind them. It drew closer behind the bikes. The men glanced back and must have sensed danger. The bikes picked up speed. One pulled ahead of the other. The car pulled alongside the slower rider. The rear window came down. Gunfire sparked from inside the vehicle. The man and his bike fell. He was probably gone before he hit the road. The faster rider disappeared down a side street.

In the darkness, I did not recognize the riders or the passengers in the car. As a scared kid, I could not even tell whether the vehicle was a Volkswagen or a Cadillac. It didn't matter. By then, I had begun to learn the street codes. And I had just witnessed what happened when people violated the rules.

That rule was clear. You don't wear the wrong color on the wrong street. Or else you pay the price. Did it make sense that young men of the same ethnicity, social conditions, and city would kill each other over the color of clothes they wore?

Some may say no. But I didn't care whether it made sense or not. It was the rule—end of story.

Growing up, I was asked several times to join gangs but sidestepped joining any of them.

"Hey, Bro," I would say. "I'm cool with you guys, but just not cut out for that."

"Man," they would respond. "With your driver's license, we could sure use you on the streets."

"I know, but I have to drive my mom around, and she keeps the keys."

This excuse was not a lie, but it helped that my mom would be in the car with me even on my drug deals. That used to end the invitations from the gangs. I was not a threat to them and kept it that way. I showed them no disrespect. I had nothing against them; I just never did fit into those groups. I was a loner. Loners don't join gangs. Gang members must trust and be loyal to each other and obey all gang rules.

My parents taught me to distrust others. In all my years in Galveston, there was only one person I completely trusted as a friend. My personality did not fit the gang profile, and I preferred it that way.

As I got deeper into distributing drugs, I had to visit other neighborhoods frequently without causing suspicion. If anyone suspected of being in a rival gang showed up in a neighborhood, there was no judge and jury. Street justice eliminated the slightest doubts. That was the tight rope I walked every day in Galveston.

Most kids who join gangs gain a sense of purpose and belonging from their new circles that they didn't get at home. I didn't get those things at home either, but my distrust of others kept me from making friendships that would have led me to gangs. Maybe those negative lessons from my parents saved me from the gang life and probably saved my life.

As I became better known for being a reliable source for drugs, the gangs left me alone. I worked hard to walk that tightrope between them without ever picking sides, and I was always careful to obey the rules about the colors I wore.

Another rule I learned when I lived in my mom's neighborhood was the value of respect, which was earned and not given. Often, the price of respect was blood.

When I was ten years old, I attended Austin Middle School at 1514 Avenue N 1/2, where my mom taught as a special-education teacher. One kid there earned a reputation for beating up other kids, and no one messed with him. That is until the day he messed with my mom.

One day at lunch in the cafeteria, he sat at my table. I was quiet until he crossed the line. He said my mom was a retard because she taught special-ed classes. I smacked him in his face with my tray until I was pulled away. That day, I realized how much rage was bottled up in me. It surprised me. I had become a product of my messed-up environment, a jumble of anger, disappointment, distrust, and fear. I had taken enough, and now, at age ten, I discovered I had the capacity to respond. To even the score. I was ready to deliver my payback to society.

My mom helped stop the fight and told me later that the kid had lost four teeth. I wasn't counting. The kid lost the bully in him that day, and I gained new status and respect in school. It was that simple. Lesson learned.

Despite my rocky relationship with my mom, it would not be the last time I would defend her. Now that I have the time to look back at the years with her, I think I defended her honor, hoping that she would return the favor with some form of motherly admiration and love. Maybe that was why I kept trying harder in more dangerous situations.

Like the night at Mr. Will's.

Mr. Will owned a gambling shack near my mother's house. He was a larger-than-life character straight out of the 1970's Motown movement. Tall, skinny, always well dressed in the Galveston heat—long sleeves, tailored slacks, and a hat. He always had a cigarette hanging from his lips. Mr. Will would sit in his canary-yellow Cadillac Seville outside his gambling shack, rocking his head to the rhythm of music blaring from his cassette player.

Meanwhile, inside his gambling shack, desperate people gambled against each other. It didn't matter to Mr. Will who won or lost. Except for a couple of armed robberies inside the shack, he always got his cut from the players. People who knew him respected him. People who did not know him learned to respect him quickly.

There were also robberies outside his single-story rundown shack. The empty lot next to his place extended into a parking lot behind the shack, where many unsuspecting first-time visitors to Galveston would be directed by phone to get their drugs from local dealers. Instead of meeting a friendly Galveston native, many would be held up at gunpoint and robbed of their last dollar.

Who would those victims turn to? The police? Mr. Will?

Of course, I am only telling you this because it's all gone now, Mr. Will, his gambling shack, and the parking lot. I am sure from the vantage point of his yellow caddie, Mr. Will saw more crime in a week than most people saw on TV in a year, but that was not his concern. You see, he also knew the rules. We all knew the rules. We didn't make them. We were all born into the game, and to win, or even just survive; you simply followed the rules.

I never judged him, and he never judged me. Mr. Will just accepted me the way I was, and I did the same for him.

I also liked Mr. Will for another simple reason. He respected me, even at age fifteen. By then, I was already roaming the streets at night, looking for trouble and finding it. Mr. Will knew me well, and despite my growing reputation for attracting bad things, we had a growing bond of friendship. He would tell me, and I believed him, that he would leave his Cadillac for me one day. Our friendship never changed in the years I knew Mr. Will. Not even after that night when again I had to defend my mother inside Mr. Will's gambling shack.

That night, my mom was sitting on the porch facing the street when a car she had never seen before pulled up and parked in a *No Parking* space in front of the house. A young man with a bad attitude got out of the car, slammed the door shut, and headed across the street toward Mr. Will's gambling shack.

My mom yelled out to him. "Hey, you can't park there!"

He turned around and shouted back. "Make me move, Bitch!"

It was loud enough for me to hear while I was inside playing a video game my dad had bought me.

In seconds, I raced across the street after him. My mom watched me leave without saying a word. I don't recall her trying to stop me or calling out to me.

This dude was already inside Mr. Will's gambling shack when I rushed past the parked yellow Cadillac and went through the door. Some people jumped from their chairs while others ran from the tables. I was right behind him when the commotion made him turn around.

When I saw the arrogance on his face, the rage within me went even higher.

I looked him in the eyes, waiting for him to make a wrong move.

He put his hands up. "What's up, Bro. I don't know who the fuck you are."

I backed up a step and got ready to fight.

Just then, Mr. Will strolled up like he was just taking a casual walk through his gambling establishment.

"What seems to be the problem, young man?" he asked.

"He just called Mom a bitch."

Mr. Will placed one hand on my shoulder. "Hey, man," he whispered to me. "That's not how we roll here. You know that. If he disrespected your mom, we got it. Now go on home, young man. I'll take care of it. Cool?"

"Cool," I said.

I understood what was about to happen and was okay with it. It was according to the rules of the streets. I never argued with the rules. I never argued with Mr. Will. I knew he would handle it. He was one of the very few people in my life I could honestly say I looked up to. He didn't scold or threaten me. His calm approach protected me from the severe consequences I would have faced in a hot-tempered moment.

Mr. Will understood street rules as I did. He grew up in the same shit. To him, this was a teaching moment. Take care of your friends. You might need them to take care of you one day. Mr. Will's way of taking care of me was to turn me around and walk me to the door.

Before my foot hit the sidewalk, I heard them fighting inside. He took care of the problem for me.

Satisfied I had restored respect for where I lived, I ran back across the street to my mom. When I walked into the house, my mom was watching TV on the living room couch. She just looked up at me and shook her head without seeming to care what had happened or could have happened with me in Mr. Will's gambling shack.

Not surprisingly, I didn't receive any love and admiration from my mother for what I did for her that night, but I never stopped trying. The need for love from one's parents is built into our DNA. It is a natural need. If parents do not fill that need, their children will learn to find it elsewhere.

That lesson helped me to become the father I am today. My biggest wish is that my children never lack what I craved growing up. My girls get my unconditional love and attention every day, without question, even though I never got it from my parents. Some days I lose focus, but I always try hard to find it again. It's a choice I make. It's a choice we can all make despite all the bullshit we faced in our younger years. My message is simple. You can change your life if you want to change it bad enough. The friends and family around you will be glad you did.

The love I give my girls is returned ten times over by the admiration and attention I get from them every day. Nothing fills my heart like my girls cuddling with me to watch TV or fall asleep. In a way, I feel sad for all that my parents missed out on. They never saw their children with love; they saw them as objects to exploit for their selfish and devious goals.

Today, my children and my wife mean more to me than I could have ever asked for. I never take them for granted and try to earn their love every single day. The point is that I have today what I did not get as a kid.

Your past does not have to equal your present. As adults, we can make that choice.

I hope this message comes across clearly.

However, all that was a long journey from where I was at age fifteen. By then, my sisters had already moved out of my mom's house. They are at least ten years older than me, and I looked up to them. I have pictures of my sisters and me, laughing and having fun. As much as they loved me and took me around with them, they were gone from the house before turning eighteen. I missed them when they left and felt a little abandoned.

Today, I understand better why they left the way they did. I know now that it was not about me; it was about them and their survival. They did what they had to do with what they had and what they knew. Today, I am at peace with their decisions, knowing they had few choices. I will always love and respect them.

The negativity and betrayals were too powerful for my sisters to remain a daily part of our family. To preserve their dignity, they had to walk away. Sad.

I wanted a family. I wanted *my* family. But a family is more than just people around you. My parents were around but never showed love to each other or their children. It might have been easier if that was where it ended. But they went further. They betrayed their children. We all face broken trust in life. The sting is worse, though, and lasts much longer when it comes from parents.

After having my children, I learned that parenting is more than just watching children grow up. It requires commitment, patience, and love—lots of it.

It's the reason I bonded so well with Nanny. She was family, and there was no mistaking how much she loved and cared for me. I felt it; I saw it, and I never doubted it. With my sisters gone, I was left with a mother in name only. She used me. I was just an object to her. There was no love between us. I felt no connection, no admiration, and no respect from her.

So, I turned to the streets for guidance. At least there, I had no expectations. I knew everyone was out for themselves. Everyone knew the game in advance. *What can I get from the other guy? What is the other guy trying to get from me?*

The only trust you had was that if the other guy saw an opening to get something from you, he would take it even if he had to hurt you or threaten to kill you. So, I remained on guard, reading between the lines, watching eyes for meanings, like in a card game. And when things went south, I was ready. I soon learned that the things I did not get from my mother, like respect, I could get from the streets.

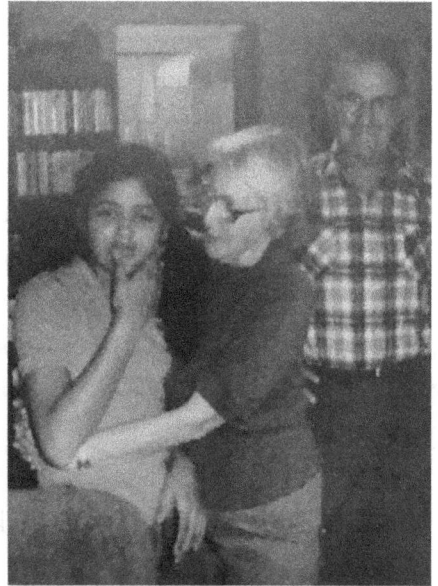

My grandmother, Nanny, created many fond memories for me and my sisters in her home on Avenue O 1/2. It's the reason I bought it to keep it in the family.

CHAPTER THREE

LIFE WITH NANNY

My paternal grandmother, Nanny, was born Mary Christine Schlatter in 1910 in Iowa. She met my grandfather in Galveston, where they married in 1940, the year before the Japanese attacked Pearl Harbor and pulled America into WWII. I never knew my paternal grandfather, Mr. William Hegmann II, but I would like to think he was a proud member of the greatest generation. These were tough people with solid principles around work and family. He was also a member of the First Lutheran Church and worked at the Oleander Warehouse.

I can only imagine that if he had been around in my youth, he and Nanny would have prevented a lot of the heartache I faced. He died at John Sealy Hospital in 1978 before I was born. He was seventy-one and left my grandmother a widow at age sixty-eight. I wish I had known him as well as I knew Nanny. She never spoke much of him, but she must have loved him. Nanny remained a widow for the rest of her life.

From my years growing up in Galveston, Nanny meant more to me than everyone I knew combined. In her house and from her heart, she gave me the haven I desperately needed to preserve my humanity. She made me feel special. She made me feel loved. She made me feel human.

Did she buy me expensive gifts and take me on expensive vacations? No, she couldn't afford it. The currency she spent on me was time, which was more valuable than any video games I got from my father or the roof over my head my mother provided. The time Nanny spent on me is still producing dividends I am now passing along to my girls, the great-granddaughters Nanny never met. If she's watching, I hope she's happy with how I am raising my children.

I remember the words she frequently said to me. "Will, you are a very special kid. You can grow up to be anything you want to become."

Little did she know she was planting seeds for my success.

Back then, I would split time between Nanny's house on Avenue O1/2 and my mother's house on Ball Street. My father lived with Nanny, so I got to do a lot of fun things with him, like riding our bikes along the seawall or shopping for video games. But there were things my father wanted us to do that would raise Nanny's suspicions. She would immediately scold him and put a stop to his plans.

Only years later, I would think back to those incidents and realize that Nanny protected me long before I was old enough to understand fully.

Because of the growing friction between my parents and me, one of my sisters, who lived about four hours away in Austin, called me to invite me to stay with her.

"You would like it here," she said. "You would have a new home, new neighborhood, new school."

"But what about Nanny?" I asked.

"You can still visit her as often as you like. Or she can come visit us."

I knew I would miss Nanny, but I looked forward to the change. I stayed with my sister and attended school in Austin for about three months.

I thought it was working out okay, but my mother complained to my sister. My new address meant my mother could not list me as a dependent on her tax returns. She insisted I return to Galveston. It was all about the money. My mother cared about three things: herself, her boyfriend, and her money.

I moved back into my mother's house in Galveston, but that soon became unbearable, so I started spending more time at Nanny's house.

My mother got her tax deduction, and I got Nanny.

I treasure the memories of my times with Nanny when we watched *The Price Is Right* together. Just the two of us. It was the perfect escape from my mom's neighborhood and the dangerous streets I had just traveled to visit Nanny. Once I was safely inside her house, Nanny would lock those deadbolts on the front door and head to the kitchen at the back of the house to prepare our favorite *Price Is Right* snack: milk-butter toast!

I could hear her footsteps creaking the wooden floors as she returned from the kitchen to the front room. She would turn on the TV and adjust her thick glasses for the event. We would sit on the couch together, snacking, mesmerized by the show. It was the perfect escape for a kid living in an imperfect reality.

Nanny and I took turns guessing the prices of the goods displayed on the show.

"I think that's about $800," Nanny would say, turning to me. "What do you think, Will?"

"Hmmm. Maybe $600."

Sometimes we got it right. Sometimes we didn't. Either way, we never lost anything. We just gained another memory of fun times together.

I enjoyed the show because it made life simple like I wished mine was. Three contestants, in silly outfits, bidding on prizes, and spinning the big wheel to the sounds of the cheering audience. Everyone was happy. Some contestants won lots of prizes: trips, shiny new cars, and appliances. Some may have lost at the game, but no one left the show with less than they came with. At least, they all left with happy memories, the sound of applause probably following them for years.

Even though Nanny was warm and loving to me, she had strict ways that made me respect her even more. She allowed me to roam the neighborhood on my bicycle by myself. I would do balancing walks and rides on yard walls in the neighborhood. I also rode around and played in the Jewish Temple Yard, close to the Ball Food Store. Nanny did most of her shopping at that store and knew the owners.

One day, the owners caught me shoplifting candy and told Nanny about it. She sent me into the backyard to cut a switch from a tree, but she never hit me. Sometimes, she scolded me for things like testing my bicycle spray paint on the cloudy window downstairs. But that was it.

My connection with Nanny was built on love and respect.

I sometimes wonder what she would have done if she knew I hid Playboy magazines and drugs in the rafters under the front patio. I am glad I never found out. My love and respect for Nanny never faded. Instead, it grew over the years as I began to appreciate how much she gave me.

I also held on to those memories of the good times with Nanny. Being in her house, protected from the world outside her door, was the most valuable gift I could ask for. Nanny gave me what every kid at that age needs: good memories and a home. The good memories reminded me that I deserved a better life. A home provides hope. The home Nanny created for me as a kid gave me the hope I needed to get to that better future. Nanny's presence in my life was my blessing.

Twenty-five years later, I still thrive on her love and psychological nourishment. It carried me through life long after she left us for good on August 30, 1997, nine days after I turned thirteen.

The news hit me hard. I was visiting my Uncle Johnny when my dad called with the sad news. His voice held no hint that he had tragic information about his mother. His words and the way he said them hit me in the gut without warning.

Twenty-five years later, that moment still rings in my ears.

Dad said, "Son, your grandmother is as dead as a doornail."

His careless words are forever etched into my memory and broke any remaining bond I felt with him as my father.

Nanny's loss left a big hole in my heart, and it changed me. But the way Dad gave me the news made it even more unbearable. I looked around my family for any recognition or sympathy I could find, but everyone around me seemed too caught up in their own mess to notice a thirteen-year-old grieving kid desperate for some compassion. The message I received was loud and clear. No one gave a shit about it.

The next day, the beautiful Princess Diana was killed in a car crash in France. The world grieved for her, and so did everyone I knew. It seemed I was the only one grieving Nanny's death. One of my sisters was out of town (she cared, no doubt), and the other two were too deep in their own painful turmoil to be supportive, or at least that is what I thought at the time. As usual, my parents were no help.

During the most painful experience of my young life, there was no one I could turn to, no one to listen to my grief.

My trust in people was already on a steep slide. After Nanny passed away, any remaining trust in my family took a big hit. Everyone for themselves. No one to depend on. If no one cared about me, why should I give a shit about anyone else?

I took on a 'kiss my ass' attitude.

To me, at that age, the world seemed cold and selfish. I began to think it was time to return the favor to the world around me. If anyone fucked with me, there would be hell to pay.

I was ready for life on the streets.

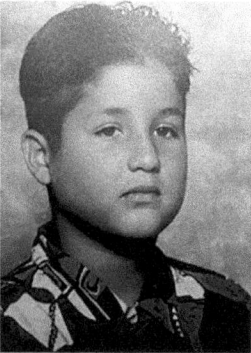

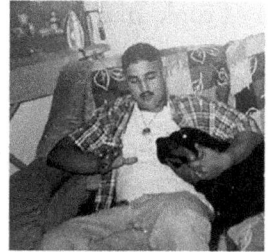

My early years changed me from a happy kid to a serious street-wise dealer. But once I learned that my past did not determine my future, I changed my life.

CHAPTER FOUR

LIFE ON THE STREETS

With my grandmother, Nanny, gone, I felt adrift. She was my rock —my source of strength and hope. To make matters worse, my father moved his girlfriend into the house. Soon, most of the furniture and anything else not bolted into the walls were gone. Even the television she and I used to watch. I believe my father and his girlfriend sold Nanny's belongings to pay for their drug habits. At least, they kept Nanny's urn in a safe corner of the closet.

I could no longer stay there, so I moved in with my mom. That did not work either. She was constantly on my case, and we just couldn't communicate. She acted like I was the reason for everything wrong in her miserable life. This would be how quickly our conversations would fall apart.

"Why don't you put away the iron and board when you're finished?" she would ask.

"I just finished. It's still hot."

"That was five minutes ago."

"Yes, Mom. It's still hot."

"I am getting real sick of you." She would glare at me. "Your sisters were always more respectful of me."

"Oh yeah? So how come all three moved away from you as fast as they could?"

"If it wasn't for you, I'd be long gone too."

"With that loser Roland?" I could be a real smart ass sometimes.

"The real loser is your father. You're headed down the same road he is."

"At least I know what road it is."

I always tried to get in the last word, and she hated me for it. She treated me like such an asshole that I asked my other sister if I could stay with her. When she agreed, I packed my things and moved in. Soon after, we started having issues at her house that caused me to move back to my mom's. When living with Mom became unbearable again, I would ask my sister if I could move back in with her.

So it went. Back and forth between my mom and my sister. With Nanny gone, I felt I no longer had a place to call home. I was always packing my bag to go from one stressful home to another. Gone were the blissful *Price is Right* days with Nanny and her tasty milk-butter toast. I was a teenager without a home and had enough of it. I was tired of pretending I could have a normal life.

Finally, one day I said, "Fuck it!"

I no longer needed my family. I always felt independent. My mother hardly provided for me as it was. True, she occasionally cooked for me, but I did all my laundry, washing, and ironing. I didn't need her companionship because she was never a mother to me. Living under her roof was not worth the hassle. So, one day, when I finally got tired of asking my sister to stay at her house, I decided not to return to my mother's house either.

Instead, I started sleeping on the streets. More accurately, I slept in parks, on benches, in alleyways, or occasionally, at a friend's house. Anywhere but my mother's house if I could avoid it. I don't even think my sisters knew. I occasionally stayed at my mom's house when she wasn't there. Otherwise, I was either in the streets or couch-hopping.

It was scary at first, but I adjusted quickly. Freedom away from my nagging mother meant more to me than worrying about the streets. However, as much as I experienced in my neighborhood under my mom's roof, the streets made it even more real. The gangs, crime, addicts, and pushers were all around. I saw many things that won't show up in this book.

Being on the streets also made me feel different about myself. People looked at me differently, too, even as a lost teenager. They looked right through me like I didn't exist in their world. Maybe it was my dingy t-shirts, shorts, and sneakers, which had become my standard street outfit.

At home, I always ironed my clothes, even t-shirts and casual shorts. But on the streets, I carried a small backpack with a couple of rolled-up changes of clothes. It did not take more than a few days for all my clothes to have that street look.

I also learned to live with very little. For one, it was not smart to sleep outdoors with jewelry on.

All I needed for a good night's sleep was a place to lay my head.

I was alone most of the time. I did not trust people, especially family. I had suffered too many disappointments and betrayals. Many nights I would lay on my back staring up at the stars reliving the good memories I had with Nanny. It would remind me how empty and meaningless my life had become without her. During those moments, the tears would flow freely.

One of my favorite places to hang out was the parking lot for Corner Bar on 53rd Street and Avenue S. The owners were cool and would let me sneak in to eat or use the restroom. It was a smokey place, with neon lights, mirrored walls, and a pool table. Most customers were as cool as the owners, and I always felt safe there.

Since I still carried a key to my mom's house, I sometimes went by when she was working at school. I would do my laundry, take a shower, and raid the refrigerator for cold leftovers. If I had time, I would take a nap on my old bed, just to remind myself what a real bed felt like.

When nights got too cold, I would sneak back into my mother's house or go to my sister Linda's. If I happened to see my mom, she never showed concern about where I was or how I was doing on the streets. She never asked what I did for food or if I needed money to feed myself. Hell, I'm not even sure she knew where I was.

I didn't need her money. I was already selling weed on a small scale, but not enough to buy fast food every day. I am sure I could have gone to my sisters, but it wasn't a comfortable option for me at that time. So, I did what I had to do, and it was a secret I kept for a long time.

I would eat food from a nearby McDonald's dumpster.

Don't get me wrong. This was not rotting food people think about when they see street people eating leftovers out of trashcans. These were wrapped hamburgers and chicken McNuggets that had been thrown away because they were not sold within a certain number of hours. The food was usually still fresh and edible, and even when other homeless people would show up for their share, there was always more food than I could eat.

I still enjoy a good McDonald's meal once in a while.

Back then, sometimes when I laid down to go to sleep on a bench, my stomach stuffed with free McDonalds, I would think how even homeless people in America could get enough to eat while children all over the world were going to sleep hungry.

What was it about this country that even the homeless lived better than most people in the world?

The one thing I never gave up on was that this country gave each of us the freedom to make choices, to either improve or destroy our lives. Yes, I saw struggle all around, but most of it was self-inflicted. No one forced the crackheads to poison their bodies and minds. No one forced the drunks to kill their livers and brain cells. I was surrounded by it all, but I chose to avoid those addictions.

I started smoking cigarettes around that time, maybe because my father made it seem casual and acceptable when I was with him. It took me years to finally quit. I never took drugs or drank alcohol that would cripple my thinking. I needed every brain cell I had to survive.

All around me, I saw people who survived better than others. Having a clear head and working hard made a difference. I saw that in successful store and bar owners and in street hustlers in the illegal drug business. I did not have the means to open a store or a bar, but I saw how easy it was to make a living by selling drugs.

My struggles made it easy for me to turn to drugs as a business. I needed the money; I thought I had a clear head, and I was willing to work hard. It was a choice that came with a high price and almost cost me my life.

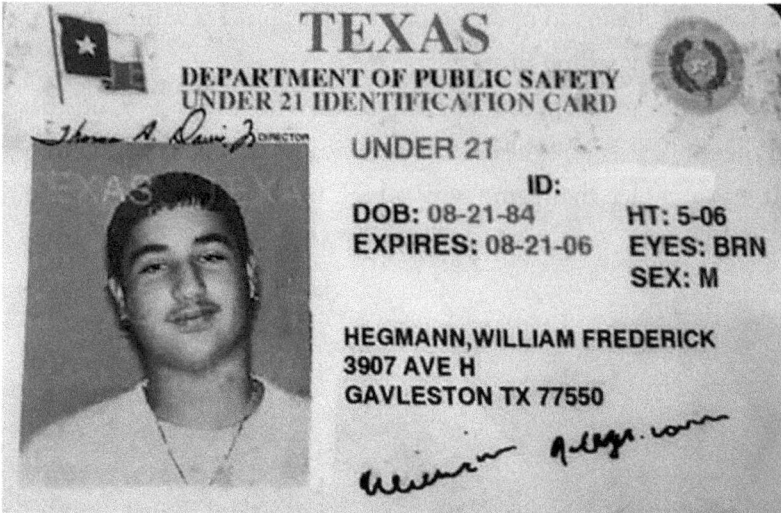

Having a driver's license at age fourteen opened up a whole new dangerous world for me.

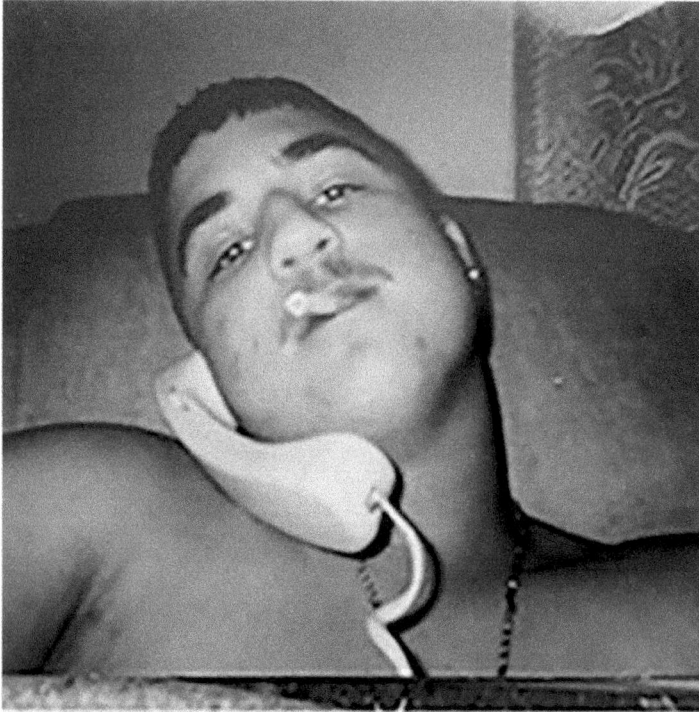

CHAPTER FIVE

GROWING UP ON THE STREETS

Having a driver's license at age fourteen opened up a whole new dangerous world for me. By then, my frequent walks and bike rides between my mother's house on Ball Street to Nanny's house on Avenue O1/2 before she passed made me a regular face in the neighborhood. I stood out. I was a Hispanic-looking kid with a German name in a hood that was eighty-percent black.

I never showed a chumpish attitude on the streets, and I never wore blue or red colors, so my travels through Bloods and Crips territories did not threaten the gangs. I once had a really nice cowboy jacket, even signed by the designer, but I never wore it. It was blue. Respect.

Don't get me wrong; I didn't avoid those colors as a favor to the gangs. I did it to avoid being shot!

Occasionally, individual thugs beat on me or stole whatever little money I had, but I never gave the gangs reason to be suspicious of me. Like most kids my age back then, I sold weed here or there to earn a few quick bucks from friends or school acquaintances, but I was never a threat to anyone, physically or as competition for their drug business. Not purposely anyway.

I soon realized that selling cocaine and pills like ecstasy brought in more money in less time than weed. I hated the effects the drugs had on people; I saw it every day. I had seen enough addicts, many who walked around, skin and bones, with paranoia, seizures, violent behavior, burnt fingertips, and missing teeth.

Some jumped off the Galveston Causeway to their deaths.

I enjoyed driving over the bridge at night while hanging out with a couple of homeboys. We would ride around Galveston at night, scoring drug deals, raising hell, or cruising and listening to music. We would drive up the causeway, blasting music and admiring the city lights in the distance, but knowing that people on drugs regularly jumped off made the drive less enjoyable.

Then there were others, especially when they were strung out on drugs, who would rob people, end up in prison, or kill themselves.

Those stories used to shock me, but they did not stop me from selling drugs.

My attitude then was cold. People chose to buy and use drugs. I chose to sell them. The consequences were not my concern. That was how the cruel world operated. People did not give a shit about me, and I did not give a shit about people. Everyone for themselves, including the drug users I saw walking around like zombies every day. That was their choice. Not mine.

Even after my mom's sister became one of the hopeless addicts, I continued to sell drugs. Unlike my mother, my aunt was warm and generous most of the time and fun to be around. I have the same birthday as her son, my first cousin, August 21st. My aunt would sometimes get us a cake to share on that date. The small gathering around the cake was the closest I had to a birthday party as a kid. Unfortunately, like most of the adults I grew up around, she also had her demons. She was a serious crack addict.

Most people confuse cocaine and crack cocaine. I am not a pharmacist, but I can tell you that cocaine is a powder, while crack cocaine comes from mixing cocaine powder with water and another substance, usually baking soda. The mixture is then boiled into a solid rock that is broken into smaller pieces and sold as crack. It is called crack because it makes a crackling sound when heated and smoked. Because of its high concentration, it is highly addictive and deadly. Most crack addicts I knew needed a fix every thirty minutes, or they would go fucking ballistic.

I was becoming accustomed to having family use me when it was convenient for them. My parents used me, so why not my aunt? That said, she wasn't one of those people. Through all the bullshit, she was someone I could call.

My cousin and I were too young to protect her from a drug deal gone wrong. I hate to say it, but the street hustlers then had better standards than those today. I read every day about innocent kids, as young as two-years-old, being killed by gunfire on the streets.

She would go out and get her fix, and once she got it, she would speed us back to her house. She would disappear into the bathroom with her crack pipe and cigarette lighter, only to reemerge on her euphoric high ten minutes later.

Some things never changed, though, and my aunt soon began stealing money from me too. That's what addicts do. Satisfying the addiction is more powerful than honesty or loyalty. She was family, and even though she stole from me and broke my trust in her, I would have always protected her in any way I could. Blood was thicker than water. It still is to me, even after all the raw betrayals from the adult family I had.

Nanny was, of course, the exception.

My aunt's drug use and the stories of people jumping off the causeway reminded me never to use the drugs I sold. I witnessed first-hand their mental and physical destruction, along with the hundreds of addicted zombies roaming the streets of Galveston.

Some have asked me a valid question: Why was I involved in selling drugs that destroyed lives, including those of friends and family? As an adult today, I feel very differently about it. It scares me to think that any of my children would ever fall victim to the stranglehold those drugs have.

Too many cases I saw hit close to home. My aunt eventually ended up in jail for possession. After that, the only friend from Galveston that I trusted and respected struggled with drug addiction for years. When I moved to Round Rock, I took him into my home to help in his recovery. He is such a loyal friend that it saddens me to see the devastation on his mind and body.

As a grown man, I can now clearly see the mistakes and bad decisions I made in my youth. At the time, I saw dealing drugs as my only option. One major reason I am writing this book is so readers can see there are always other options.

As a teenager, I did not see them. It was easy to rationalize selling drugs without feeling guilty. It was one of those street realities I was born into. It was my world. Despite the risks of being arrested, getting shot, and spending years in jail, selling drugs was the first career choice for most youth I knew in Galveston. It was easy to get into it. Customers were already set to break down my door to buy the drugs they needed. I did not create the drug trade, and it would have gone on with or without me.

The amount of money was also a huge temptation. I made more money in some weeks than professional career people made in a month. I did not keep all the money. My mother shared in my profits and never once discouraged me from participating in the illegal drug trade. My aunt, without knowing it, taught me how easy the money was when I saw how much she bought and how easy it was for her to purchase.

Even as my childhood fear of my aunt's crack addiction faded in time, I kept calculating the potential profits I'd make doing it myself. I was not the sharpest student in school, but mathematics was always my strongest interest. Numbers came naturally to me. Maybe I was born with a photographic memory for numbers. I memorized drug weights, dollars per unit, and potential profit. When I combined my interest in mathematics with the money I could earn on the streets, I became hooked. Not on the drugs but the money.

I figured if I bought seven grams of crack for about two hundred dollars, I could break it into thirty-five rocks at twenty dollars apiece. That's seven hundred dollars. I could easily triple my money in one day.

From the number of deals I observed around my neighborhood, I quickly realized I could make a $500 per day profit in the crack cocaine business. That's all I thought about all day. How much would I make if I sold this much at this price? If I doubled the number of sales, how much would I make? The possibilities seemed endless.

At age fourteen, I was ready.

I started selling weed and soon moved up to cocaine and crack cocaine. My biggest breakthrough came with ecstasy pills. Easier to hide. Easier to transport. Easier and safer to sell. Easy profit.

I didn't know then that I was beginning to build a pattern for future business success. It meant knowing the product, understanding my clients, target marketing, calculating the numbers, and, yes, practicing ethics.

Ethics in the illegal drug business?

What a fucking joke, right? It might be hard for most people to understand, but ethics played a huge role in my growth from a small-time weed pusher at age fourteen to a five-figure drug distributor on the streets of Galveston. My suppliers had to trust that I would keep my word and pay on time. My customers had to trust the quality of my product. They had to know I would deliver when and how I said I would.

Practicing street ethics meant my word, money, and drugs could be trusted.

Reliability counts as much in illegal drug trafficking as in a legitimate business. In a legal business, you lose profit if you fail your suppliers and customers. In the drug game, if you fail your suppliers and customers, you could lose your life. You could also lose your life if a street competitor wants to cut in on your illegal drug profits. Survival on the streets meant protecting your profits and your life. It was a daily struggle.

I did not learn win-win in an elite business school up north. I learned it on the streets, in the drug business. As a teenager, I earned more than most overeducated professionals with college degrees.

I am not knocking college education. As you will soon read, education was my ticket out of my dark past. The point I want to make, especially for the benefit of young people, is that success on the streets requires many of the same business approaches used in the legal business world. Take your business mindset and desire for success into the real business world. You will sleep better at night, without the risks, fear of prison, or worse, and without the guilt that you're destroying human life.

I hope this lesson carries over to young men and women who are risking their lives and freedom selling dangerous drugs on the streets today. There are better options in the world of business.

But back to my story.

I used to make a killing selling pills at 'rave' parties. Someone once told me that the word came from the French word, *raver*, which means "to show signs of madness or delirium." Why anyone would use drugs that push them to madness and hallucinations is beyond me. Nevertheless, I did not judge them. They did not judge me. I did not care. They were happy to pay me for the pills, and I was happy to supply them. That's where it ended. I never took them.

Rich kids would get off techno music and ecstasy pills at these raves. They would dance and sweat all night, smiling like they were in heaven. The pills helped take them to a higher level. I read in the papers that some who took more than they should never either died or were never the same from their highs.

I remember attending such an event one night with my best friend. Business was so good we could barely keep up. We kept running back and forth to the car to drop off stacks of cash and get more pills. By the end of the night, we had sold out and earned more than most executives make in a month! Exhausted from running in the humidity all night, we counted the money listening to DJ Screw:

Got the Heart Of A Hustler (Heart Of A Hustler)

I Got The Mind Of A G (Mind Of A G)

I'm Out Here Getting My Paper (Getting My Paper)

So Don't Fuck With Me (Don't Fuck With Me)

I Wake Up In The Morning When The Sun Rise

I Got My Mind On That Paper Chasing Them Dollar Signs

It Ain't No Time For Resting Or Taking Naps

I Gotta Have Some Counting Up All Paper Stacks

I Got Dreams And Aspirations Of Balling Big

I Want A Crib In Them Hills Where Kobe Live

And I Can Get It If I put My Grind To It

Before going further, let me make something very clear. Today, as the happy husband of a beautiful wife and a lucky father of her son and young, loving daughters, I am not proud of any of this shit. It would pain me beyond belief if any of my children were to experience an ounce of the struggle, bad decisions, and risks in their own lives. Children need to be children. They need attentive parents in their lives. They need structure and guidance. Without any of this, things can turn bad very quickly. I know it from experience.

GROWING UP ON THE STREETS

If this book changes one mind, a parent or a child, then maybe I'll save a life.

It's sad and painful to admit that my parents were great examples of what NOT to do and be with children. They divorced when I was a baby, but that was the least of the problems that awaited me as a child. Like I said earlier, maybe there was a time my mother had a natural love for me as a newborn. I do not remember her expressing or showing love for my sisters or me. I still remember bike riding with my dad along the sea wall and sitting down with him for a restaurant meal. I looked up to him as a kid, but that quickly shattered when I found out who he really was.

Don't get me wrong. I was not some spoiled brat that was given everything and is now turning against my parents. I have seen that with other kids, and it sickens me. I sincerely wish my parents were happier people with or without me. As it turned out, they both had serious personal flaws. Their demons stood in the way of being parents. I just happened to be born to them and was exposed to their misery.

I'll have more on my father later, but for now, I want to clarify that the problem with my mother was not that she was physically absent in my life. As I said, I lived in her house mostly when I was not at Nanny's. Since my mother had heart issues, I started driving her around as a young teenager. As weird as it seems, that helped me build a new relationship with her. But not the typical mother-son relationship.

It might sound cold, but my mother was always more interested in money than her children. When my drug deals started to bring in money that I shared with her, she saw an opportunity to work with me, even when I protested against her doing so.

"Mom, this is risky for you," I said. "I can give you money, but you don't have to come with me."

She was straight up. "Police are always looking for young people driving around in fancy cars," she told me. "They don't have time to mess with a teenager driving his mother around in a beat-up Toyota Camry."

"I still don't like it."

"Don't forget, I am still your mother. I know what's best."

She was right about our mother and son 'cover' when we drove around getting my stashes. We never got caught.

I guess I used her too.

Maybe it also helped that, besides my gold chain, I was always in a t-shirt, jeans, and sneakers. Nothing about me, my mom, or our car looked suspicious. We made the perfect team. She drove with me on most of my big deals. Sometimes we carried enough crack and pills to bring six figures on the street between Galveston and Houston. She walked into abandoned warehouses with me to meet buyers and sellers, all armed and ready to shoot it up with anyone suspicious. To be honest, I am ashamed of these moments. None of my sisters or family knew about them as far as I know. Many will hear it for the first time if they read this book.

When ecstasy became more popular, we drove around with thousands of those pills in the car. Easier to carry. Faster money. My mom gladly became my cover for my drug deals because she shared in the profits. It didn't have shit to do with love and affection. It had nothing to do with her bonding with her son. She never discouraged me. She never expressed concern that I might be caught and sent to prison for years. Or worse. Drug dealers were shot regularly in Galveston. It was about the money. Period. My mother's only concern was that my drug activities brought her a steady flow of money so she could spend it on Roland or whatever else she did without me.

My drug deals didn't always go well. One night, I got a call that a supplier would be stopping by my house to make an unscheduled delivery. I did not like doing deals like that, especially at my home. I didn't want shady characters I couldn't trust, knowing where I lived and what I did.

But I made an exception to my rule that night.
It nearly cost me my life.

I felt uneasy as soon as the brand-new Lexus with shiny rims pulled up in front of the house at one o'clock in the morning. Two guys stepped out of the car. A Mexican dude and a white guy. Both were dressed up—flashy rings, huge chains, and polished shoes that shined in the streetlight.

These were not smart guys. They were fuckups. Flashy and stupid.

I stepped outside in my t-shirt, shorts, and flip-flops. I walked down the narrow walkway toward the street gate with my gun.

The idiots stood on the sidewalk in loud-ass conversation, enough to wake up the whole damn street. When I approached them, they kept looking around and acting jittery.

Suddenly, cop cars with flashing lights and sirens raced down the street from both directions. The cars screeched to a halt around the Lexus, and cops jumped out.

The two idiots just stood there watching like innocent bystanders watching a drug bust.

I stepped back a few paces into my yard, unsure who they were coming for. I slowly made my way back into the darkness and into the house.

The cops pulled the two aside, searched the cars, and arrested them. I never saw them again. Thankfully, the cops never came for me. They may not have had a warrant, and I was already back inside.

My mother watched the whole episode from the window. She was aware of the risks I faced every day, but as long as I gave her money from my deals, she considered herself my partner. She never hinted that she was concerned I could be in a drug bust like the one she saw from her window that night. She really did not seem to care what could happen to me on my daily drug deals, with or without her.

Despite my extra time with Mom, the emptiness inside me worsened. As time passed, I saw less and less of my father, partly because I also started to see and learn things about him that filled me with rage. He was not the hero I thought he was—far from it.

My father was a drug user, a petty thief, and worse.

When I turned fifteen, I received news that my father had been arrested for sexual assault crimes. The victims were my sisters.

My world and my life came crashing down again.

As a kid, I loved and adored my sisters (Lilia,Linda, and Krista), but didn't quite know how to show it at that age. I love them more today. Lilia took me to catch my first fish!

CHAPTER SIX

IS LIFE WORTH LIVING?

The news that my father had been arrested for abusing my sisters devastated me. I never felt so low, angry, or let down. Instead, I felt useless and helpless. As their only brother, I should have been there to defend the sisters I loved so much. But how could I have known since all this happened when I was too young to understand? I don't even think I was alive when some of it unfolded.

When the news came out, I recalled an incident when I was about seven or eight years old. Dad and I had just returned from a bike ride, hot and sweating. We were standing in the living room while Nanny was in the kitchen.

He looked at me and asked what I thought was a strange question. "You want to go take a shower with your daddy?"

Nanny stormed in from the kitchen. "The boy is old enough to take his own shower," she yelled. "Leave him alone!"

There was no mistaking her tone. She was highly pissed at him.

Did Nanny know her son was a monster and was just protecting me from my father? Did she know he had a dark, uncaring part of his personality that could make him turn on his children?

When I thought about the things my sisters must have gone through with my father, it all began to make sense. They avoided him during my youth and never said much about him. They also didn't ask me many questions about him either. They must have carried a lot of anger at my mother for not protecting them. I am not accusing her of knowing about it and ignoring it. I know from experience that even when my mother was physically present, she could be a thousand miles away mentally.

She was never emotionally connected to us. If my sisters showed signs of sexual abuse, my mother would have never seen them. As a mother, she was as helpless to them as she was to me. It also made sense why all three packed up and left my mother's house as soon as possible, like they were escaping a trap.

This was a battle my sisters knew they had to fight alone, with all the pain, anger, and guilt bundled up inside them.

I had also seen other signs that my father was not the man I idolized as a child. He tried to hide the telltale signs of drug use, but my experience on the streets taught me what to look for—sleeplessness, changing moods, and desperation for money. Maybe his need to feed his growing drug habit pushed him toward crime. He became a petty thief and tried to get me to team up with him.

When Nanny died, my father and his girlfriend sold everything in the house that wasn't attached. When I last visited the house, just months after Nanny passed away, the only thing I could identify as hers was the urn where my dad kept her ashes in the closet.

The news of my dad's arrest and all those fucking memories came crashing down on me all at once. I tried to cry out the pain, but like a dam, it refilled as quickly as I let out some of my emotions.

At age fifteen, I decided that life was not worth living.

I went to a nearby Walmart and bought the largest bottle of aspirin I could find on the shelf. Then, I headed to my favorite hangout, Corner Bar on 53rd Street and Avenue S.

I sat on the wall behind the bar and started to swallow handfuls of aspirin. Each time I recalled the painful shit my parents shoveled into my life and my sisters' lives, the more pills I shoved into my mouth and down my gut.

> Swallowing the pills felt easier when I thought
> I might see Nanny again that night if I made it
> to heaven where she deserved to be.

I had been born into a life of shitty parents, in a shitty reality. I had been given very few choices. Even then, all my options sucked. I no longer attended school regularly. I walked the streets during the day, selling drugs to keep money in my pocket. Even with drug money, deep inside, I never felt worthy of having more. I wasted a lot of money on crazy shit. Many nights, my meal was a McDonald's hamburger from a dumpster, and my bed was a hard park bench with no blankets or pillows.

I had no friends or family I trusted. I hated being around my mother. My sisters and I hardly spoke since my mother poisoned our relationships and turned us on each other. My father was going to jail for a long time, I hoped. And the emptiness I felt after losing Nanny felt too painful to heal.

I had no one. I had nothing. I was nothing. My past was a wreck, and my future looked worse than I had ever imagined.

That night outside Corner Bar, I felt I was making the only choice that was truly mine. It was the only choice I had left. I wanted it to be my permanent cure from everything that fucked with my mind every day and night.

If I died, I would never again feel like the only Mexican-looking kid in the neighborhood. I would never again have to fear the gangs or worry about wearing blue or red colors. I would never again have to carry a weapon to feel safe in my city. I would never again feel the anger that always had me one second from hurting someone really badly.

Dying felt like the easiest solution.

However, it was not to be.

I knew a guy in the neighborhood who was one of the few living a straight life, as difficult as that was in Galveston. He became a police officer and soon started patrolling the streets as a trainee. That night, he just happened to be walking by the Corner Bar. I don't remember what time or what I was doing when he saw me. I might have been passed out on the wall. He looked at me and instantly knew I needed medical help fast. He got an ambulance to rush me to the hospital.

They pumped out the contents of my stomach and saved my life.

But my condition was serious, and my recovery was slow because of potential damage to my liver. They kept me in the hospital for ten days, I think. I spent many hours replaying my life in my mind. All the shit I was going through. The disappointments. The betrayals. I couldn't trust even my own family.

**During that time in hospital,
not a single family member came to see me.**

**The only one who had a valid reason not to
visit was my father because he was under arrest.**

But I am hardly making excuses for him. The things he did and said destroyed any respect I had left for him, and I didn't want him there anyway.

As bad as things were then, another bombshell awaited me years later.

A total stranger contacted me out of the blue one day.

"Mr. Hegmann?" The woman sounded serious.

"Yes, how can I help you?"

"Do you know the name Mary Christine Hegmann?"

"Yes, of course," I said. "She was my grandmother, Nanny."

"I have something that belongs to her and was hoping to return it to a family member."

Still not sure what she had, I quickly responded. "Thank you. I'll be glad to make arrangements to get it. What is it?"

The stranger explained that someone found a plastic bag among discarded trash during an organized road clean-up in Galveston. Inside the bag was a card with Nanny's name.

"I have the plastic bag," the woman said. "I am sorry to say I think it might be your grandmother's ashes."

My heart fell to a new low. I knew my father and his girlfriend Patty sold everything in the house, probably to support their drug habit. I remember seeing Nanny's urn in the empty house the last time I visited him.

Those fuckers probably sold Nanny's urn and threw away her ashes like trash on the roadside!

It hurts to think my father could be so cold and uncaring to his mother, even after she passed away. Then, I remember how he treated his children like trash, too.

I started this book saying I was not supposed to make it to twenty years old. That's no exaggeration. I know many others who died as teenagers. And it's not only in Galveston. Just turn on the news, and you will see story after story, day after day, in city after city across America, of young lives wasted and ended on the streets.

Almost 700,000 kids under eighteen were arrested in 2019 for everything from murder, drugs, and weapons— you name it.

I already told you I like working with numbers, but not these kinds of numbers. It's too close to home. These numbers remind me about my teenage years and the life of crime that finally caught up with kids I knew. Hell, somebody even wrote a song called Teenage Crime, about the lucky ones still alive:

IS LIFE WORTH LIVING?

We don't sleep when the sun goes down

We don't waste no precious time

All my friends in the loop

Making up for teenage crime

YouTube has some interesting reviews on the song. Some people just repeated the lyrics, probably because it was true about their friends. One person cut to the chase. He just wrote RIP.

Another study showed that most of these kids came from abusive homes, with no positive adults in their lives.

I know these kids because I was one of them. I came from the homes they lived in. I walked the streets they walked. I slept on the park benches they slept on. I broke the same laws they broke. I was just one of the lucky ones. I was never jailed.

Maybe I was lucky for a reason. Perhaps the reason is for me to write this book. I want desperately to save as many lives as possible from that way of life. I am not proud of many things I did on the streets. At my age at the time, I knew nothing different. It was all I knew. I did not ask to be born into a broken family in a fucked-up city. I did not choose my rules of survival. I cannot change that past. All I can hope to do now is pass along what I learned so that others can make better choices.

By age seventeen, I had seen enough, done enough, and escaped enough close calls to know that I would not make it to age twenty if I did not change.

My Uncle Greg, who owned an air conditioning business in Houston, encouraged me to get my Heating, Ventilation, and Air Conditioning

(HVAC) certificate. We weren't close, but I remember his advice. He suggested that I register in a government training program called Job Corps.

I did not make my decision until I was lying in another hospital bed, staring at the ceiling again after another close call with death.

First day - February - 12-02

Ending Date = Chris 1820.00
MASON in TRUSK

A1 - D. 2.00
and vanilla

Ugly man
5.00

C $20/50

Ugene
10.00

Bob starkman
You Should Never get a second chance To
make a First impression!

Things you need To make a good First
Impression.

1: EYe contact 2: Greetings 3: Clothes
4: Smile 5: Posture 6 Attitude
Research on the company Before you
go For an Interview
6: hand shake - very important to do in interview
7 Always maintain EYe contact But Do not
over do it,
7: social skills

WEEK 2: chores

Affirmation: I will be open To change!

I came here to change From the way I was Before

My first days at Job Corps.

(Left) Change was not always easy: my customer list and payment due for contrabrand cigarettes and alcohol.

(Right) But I was focused on my goal as the last two lines show: *'I will be open to change'* and *'I came here to change from the way I was before.'*

CHAPTER SEVEN

HOW JOB CORPS HELPED CHANGE MY LIFE

One day, as I was preparing to leave Galveston for Job Corps, I decided to get a haircut. That's where I was, sitting in a barbershop chair on September 11, 2001, when terrorists slammed planes into the Twin Towers, the Pentagon, and a Pennsylvania field, killing thousands of innocent people.

It enraged everyone, including me.

The world was changing before my eyes. It reminded me how short life can be and why it was vital for me to change my own life instead of waiting for change to come knocking on my door. The passengers on those planes no longer had the opportunity to change their lives. At least I still had a chance.

Enrolling in Job Corps during a national emergency seemed like a small decision, but it changed my life for the better. Job Corps is a federally funded educational program that provides free opportunities for young people sixteen to twenty-four years old. Its mission is to improve the quality and satisfaction of lives with vocational and academic training. In other words, they taught new skills so students like me would become productive members of society.

At seventeen years old, all I understood was drugs, guns, and anger. I needed Job Corps badly.

There are more than one hundred campuses across the country. I enrolled at the Gary Job Corps Center in San Marcos, Texas. Covering 800 acres, it is the largest Job Corps center in the United States. At the time, I felt it was my best chance to get out of Galveston alive.

To be accepted at Job Corps, I had to meet basic requirements. One was that I did not display behavioral problems, require institutional supervision, or owe court fines. Lucky for me, I survived my years in Galveston without a single police or court incident. Maybe it was luck. Perhaps it was Nanny looking over her grandson. Whatever it was, I met these primary qualifications.

Another requirement was that I had to come from a low-income family. That was easy enough. My parents never had money, at least not money earned from a legal job that I knew of. Even though I made more money on the streets in a month than the Job Corps administrators evaluating my application would earn in a year, no one would know that. That kind of money never shows up at the IRS. So yes, I met another key requirement.

Job Corps also required additional technical training, education, counseling, or assistance to complete schoolwork or find and keep a job. Check, check, check. I was all of the above. I was a high school dropout and never held a real job. Drug-delivery tactics and street-survival skills were not on the list of respected achievements in this new world I was hoping to escape into. So, bingo, I was accepted.

I enrolled in the HVAC program as my Uncle Greg suggested. Since I had not yet earned a high school diploma, I signed up to attend classes for my high school equivalency diploma, commonly known as the GED.

I was ready to start a new chapter in my life on my first day at the Gary Job Corps Center. I realized this was an opportunity, not a guarantee. For it to work, I had to work. That's the way life fucking works! So, I rolled up my sleeves and prepared to face my new life as a student.

I still have my notes from my first day at Job Corps. The instructors laid out the rules for dress code and seating arrangement. But they also talked about things that make a good first impression in the business world, like eye contact, posture, and attitude. Job Corps lessons were beginning to sound like some of the same lessons I learned on the streets.

The instructors also explained a concept called affirmation—a positive or negative statement that affects how you act when repeated.

By week two, I had chosen a positive affirmation for my future. I wrote it in a notebook that I still have: "I will be open to change. I came here to change from the way I was before." It is incredible how this affirmation guided everything I have done and accomplished since Job Corps.

Physically, the Job Corps center had everything you would find on a university campus. Dorms, cafeteria, swimming pool, gym, library, laundry, and even a post office and a bank. Everything was clean and orderly.

I was on the road that would leave my past behind and lead me to a bright new future. Or so I thought!

I didn't realize at the time that while I was leaving Galveston's dangerous streets behind, many Job Corps students were leaving their troubled gang-infested neighborhoods in other cities for the same reasons.

While the center had students like all campuses, Job Corps students were not always the type you find at a regular university. Many Job Corps students during my time carried street grudges many miles long—some stretching from Louisiana to Houston. Much of the tension among the students was caused by confrontations between Louisiana and Houston gangs. I wanted none of it. I had left my shit behind in Galveston. Plus, I reasoned, I was not from Houston.

Not so quick!

The Louisiana boys could tell Houston students by how they spoke. And guess what? To those fuckers, I sounded like I was from Houston! So, on my first day, trouble came knocking on my dorm-room door. Instead of reading a book on HVAC or solving some math problems, I had to revert to my street ways.

That really pissed me off!

Here's how it went down. I shared my dorm room with a few other students. We had bunk beds, desks, chairs, and ceiling-high closets. Not much more, except an ironing board and iron. I was never into fancy clothes, but whatever I wore had to be clean and pressed—even my t-shirts and shorts. Unlucky for the Louisiana boys, they made their unwelcomed visit to my dorm when I was in my room alone, doing my ironing on my first night at Job Corps.

Three Louisiana boys barged in through the doorway and looked around to ensure I was alone. Two shouldered one of the closets across the floor to block the door while the third charged at me.

Big mistake.

I grabbed my iron and put it on his neck and chest. The second guy got the iron to his chest. Within minutes, all three had fled out the window.

**Galveston street rules had followed me to San Marcos.
Respect is earned, many times, with blood and pain.
My reputation was sealed on day one.**

Other Galveston habits also followed me. I had spent more than three years in the drug business, mainly as a profitable distributor. While I was determined to change my life and leave drugs behind, I kept my business mindset.

I switched from crack and ecstasy on the streets of Galveston to alcohol and cigarettes in Job Corps.

Big problem: Job Corps has a zero-tolerance policy for drugs, alcohol, and tobacco.

My experience in Galveston taught me that if people desperately need a product, they will find a way to get it. If it is forbidden by law, they will pay even more for it. I never took an economics class, but I learned about supply and demand on the streets.

In my Job Corps classes, I heard people asking where they could buy a carton of cigarettes, a six-pack of beer, or a bottle of alcohol. I saw lots of money going into the pockets of a handful of students willing to break campus rules for needy customers. Job Corps not only provided me the opportunity to gain new skills and education but also presented me with a business opportunity.

I decided to enter the tobacco and alcohol business at the Gary Job Corps Center because I needed money to live.

I approached this new challenge with a business mindset. I knew supplies were limited because they were not allowed on campus. Customers were plentiful and willing to pay a premium to anyone who could deliver, so that was the easy part. The main challenge I faced was that I was not old enough to buy alcohol.

Also, regular searches by campus gate security led to busts that resulted in the loss of money and expulsion from Job Corps. Even if I successfully got it onto campus, I had to find somewhere to store it.

As a businessman, I had to come up with a plan.

First, how do I get alcohol and cigarettes? I was not much of a drinker. I couldn't tell the difference between Jim Beam and Jack Daniels. Plus, I was just beginning to develop the cigarette habit, so I didn't know the difference between Marlboro and Winston cigarettes.

I didn't care about those details. Just like I avoided taking the illegal drugs I sold in Galveston, I realized I would have to exercise the same discipline with my supplies. Dipping into my products would weaken my mind and my profits.

But first, I had to recruit some older students as partners who could legally buy the products for me. I simply cut them in on a piece of the action.

The next challenge was getting the alcohol and cigarettes onto campus without getting caught. Gary Job Corps fits into the wide triangle where Camino Road and Arnold Avenue cross. To the south, an old train track made up the third boundary. The entire campus was closed in by a chain-linked fence. The main gates were too risky, with watchful security guards always on alert for incoming contraband. Any opening in the fence I could find on the main streets was also too obvious and visible to regular foot and automobile traffic.

That left the train-track boundary.

One day, I scouted the area behind some bushes along the train-track boundary and found a narrow opening in the fence. It was just wide enough for me to squeeze through with a backpack. Well away from security guards, on the far side from the main gates, it was also hidden from the street and out of view of any nosey neighbors. The pieces of my plan were coming together.

Finally, I had to construct a hidden storage area in my dorm room. During my drug days, I stashed the pills and powder behind a baseboard in my room at my mom's house. But the baseboards in the dorms were not that easy to disturb without making it evident to unwelcomed visitors. The closets, though, were a different matter. I easily removed the baseboard and adjusted a false flooring beneath the closet, creating enough space for six-packs of beer, bottles of alcohol, and cartons of cigarettes.

On a typical shopping day, I would walk or drive to the store with my friend, who was old enough to buy alcohol and cigarettes legally. He would make the purchases with money I gave him, including a reasonable commission. He did not want to risk helping me smuggle it into the center by way of the back fence, so I would walk alone down the old train track with my new purchases stacked in my backpack. Then I would make my way across the shrubs to the back fence area behind the bushes. Careful not the break bottles or shake the beer, I would squeeze through the opening with my backpack.

Since everyone carried bags and backpacks all over campus, I fit right in once I cleared the fence.

In no time, I became one of the leading suppliers of contraband goods in the Gary Jobs Corps Center.

Despite the early clash with the Louisiana boys, the rest of my time at Job Corps went smoothly. I studied a lot. Instead of cutting crack, I was turning book pages. I learned a lot, which helped me develop a sense of purpose and build my self-confidence. On the streets of Galveston, I was good with numbers, calculating cocaine weights, cutting crack, and counting pills and money. As a student at Job Corps, I excelled in math and other subjects.

I earned my GED and HVAC certificates.

A new part of me came alive, and I began to respect and admire the changes I saw in myself. Gradually, my Galveston memories began to fade—just a little. I now had a future I could work hard at during the day.

Without having to worry about sleeping at night. Without having to look over my shoulder. Without having to team up with my mother. I began to see the light at the end of the tunnel, and it looked promising.

The Job Corps experience, my on-campus business, and the official program taught me a lot that I took into the legal business world—the discipline to study, plan, and schedule my time. It added structure to my life and taught me to apply principles that could help me build a successful future. I learned that success is not accidental. It is built on hard work and dedication.

I also discovered that none of those traits were new to me. I had been using them on the streets of Galveston for years. Now, I could sharpen those approaches in lawful efforts. It lifted a burden off my mind. I would no longer have to look over my shoulder wherever I went. I no longer had to be on high alert every day for cops or ruthless competitors. I began to feel a sense of freedom I had lost as a kid.

I was ready to take on the world and show what I was really made of.

I tell my Job Corps story for two reasons. First, because it was true. Second, I want readers, especially young, troubled youth involved in the drug game, to understand something that could turn their lives around in a heartbeat. The skills they use to earn money dealing drugs on the streets can be used in the legitimate business world without the real risk of spending the rest of their fucking life in jail.

I came from nothing. Nevertheless, I have a new life today with some basics I learned along the way. I never got a handout. Job Corps was an opportunity. I was ready for it, and I took it. Simple. People who believe they need handouts are weak-minded individuals who spend more time focusing on other people's businesses instead of building their own. They believe only people with privilege and handouts make it in life. I call bullshit on that. All they must do is focus some basics and energy on themselves and their business. Period.

In all my life, I never made excuses. Maybe it was a good thing I had parents who didn't give a shit about listening to anything I had to say. They never listened or cared enough to encourage excuses from me.

Whether it was legal or not, I did what I had to do at the time and let the chips fall where they may.

Was I ever scared? Hell yes. Life is not always sweet and comfy. When shit comes your way, you deal with it using what you have at the time. That's it. Everything has risk, but excuses don't make it go away.

I sometimes watch the talking idiots on TV feeding junk into gullible young minds. Politicians get off on telling people their success in life depends on electing them to office so that they can pass this law or that law, support this program or that program, or give this handout or that handout.

Bullshit. People who fall for that are settling for crumbs. Politicians can't lead you to success. Politicians make promises that give them more power. Their skill is making people believe they care more about them than they do themselves. In the end, the politicians walk away with more power and more money, leaving the people wishing for the next politician that comes along with better promises, like a drug addict.

That's exactly what drugs do to people. They can only see the next high. Once they get it, they keep coming back for the next fix.

Success is from the inside out, and only one person can lead you to success—You.

Only one person can lead you to failure—You.

Even when given opportunities like Job Corps, about two out of every ten students fail to finish the program. Why?

The biggest hang-up most people have is about their past. They had a rotten childhood, bad parents, attended a bad school or were discriminated against. On and on and on with any excuse they could pull out of their ass.

Bullshit again. Your past doesn't make your future. Your decision to let your past influence your future makes it so.

George Foreman could have made all the same excuses, coming from the streets of Houston as a troubled youth. Instead, he also changed his life in Job Corps, which is just one of many opportunities available for young people to change their lives.

But opportunities themselves don't change lives. People must first decide to change. Then they must engage the opportunities. Nothing happens without effort.

Your decision to kiss your past goodbye will free you from it. It takes effort, but my life proves it can be done. Today, my future looks nothing like my past.

Again, I am not saying look what I did. I am saying to anyone who wants to listen to me or read this book, look what YOU can do.

In the last five years, my business partner Patrick Connell and I built a successful real estate training program, *The Social Agent*. We have trained more than 48,000 real estate agents in ten countries. These people can now use the tools we developed to build successful lives. In addition to our home base in Texas, we are expanding our brokerage into six more states. Discipline and hard work got us there.

When I open my soul here to tell young people about where I started and where I am today, it is not hot air. I lived it. I know it. All it takes is the decision to change and the determination to keep doing something each day to make you a better person.

The pieces will come together in time.

True, my first big step away from Galveston at age seventeen was Job Corps. Yes, Job Corps was an opportunity, but it did not hand me success. It did not make me who I am today. You can lead a horse to water but can't force it to drink. I was thirsty for change, success, and a break. First, I had to recognize opportunity and make it a part of my mindset. I had to apply it and had to work it.

Business success can't be handed to anyone. It is a choice, and I chose to embrace the opportunities Job Corps presented me. I chose to turn that opportunity into the bridge that allowed me to walk away from my dead-end past to a brighter future. I chose to read the textbooks. I chose to listen to my teachers. I chose to leave the regrets of my past behind and focus on my future instead.

I made many decisions in my youth, most of which were lawless and risky. The decision to turn the Job Corps experience into a building block for my future was different. It was probably the first real decision I made that did not come with regrets.

With my GED and an HVAC certification, I felt prepared for the next step on my journey to put the Galveston experience behind me.

When I left Job Corps in 2003, the country was still in shock from the 9/11 attacks. Many young people were enlisting in all branches of the military to join the fight against terror. About three percent of Job Corps graduates join the military.

I began to think that joining the Navy after graduation would be a great step into my future and a giant leap away from Galveston.

But first, I had to return to my hometown one last time.

For the first time I met someone I wanted to get to know and I
wanted with me. Believe it or not,
after just a month,
was I in love?

Yes!

CHAPTER EIGHT

HOW COLLEGE AND DELL PREPARED ME FOR BUSINESS SUCCESS

Graduating from Job Corps two years after enrolling gave me a real sense of accomplishment. I had worked hard, studied hard, and it paid off. This reinforced my belief in myself and my ability to make the changes needed to build a solid future. I felt a natural high, not the high so many people try to get from drugs or alcohol but something else that is hard to explain.

**It was a high of achievement.
I was hooked, and I wanted more.**

So, I decided to join the Navy. The timing was right. America was riding a new wave of patriotism to combat terrorism around the world. Young Americans like me were fighting in Afghanistan and Iraq. I felt it was an opportunity to escape Galveston and make a difference in my country.

After graduation, I returned to Galveston to complete the applications and testing for joining the Navy. I was told it would take a couple of months, so I used that time to clean up some unfinished business from my past. I had about 5,000 ecstasy pills still hidden behind the baseboard in my mother's house.

One of the very few people I call a true friend decided to drive me one night to make my final delivery. I didn't want to, but I needed money before going off on my own for good.

We were almost at our drop-off location when police sirens and flashing lights raced up behind us. I felt like my life had come to an end. But the worst part was that I had taken my friend with me. How could this happen to me now? Just as I was about to walk away from my past, it came crashing down on me.

We pulled over and were taken away.

At age eighteen, it had to be one of the lowest points of my life, among many other low points I had experienced up to that point.

In addition to losing my best friend, I mentally kissed goodbye to my fucking Job Corps success and my Navy plans.

But miracles of miracles, I was released. To this day, I don't have all the details. As it was later explained, my best friend took the hit for me. He pled a deal so I could walk without me even knowing it. He must have known how determined I was to change my life. He took full responsibility for the pills. I signed what I thought was a confession, but it was something entirely different. If I knew what I was signing, I wouldn't have, and we'd have done time together. I would likely still be in there.

I have never forgotten his sacrifice for me, and I could never repay him enough for saving my life and future.

I struggle every day to do right by him and for my family. I felt like I had been given a second, or maybe a third, fourth, or fifth chance in life. I had lost count and was not about to take any more chances.

While waiting for the Navy application process, I turned to a counselor who had been encouraging me to go to college. She did not discourage me from joining the Navy; she just explained the advantages of getting a college education, especially since I had done so well in Job Corps.

I was convinced.

She helped me with my college application and registration. In the Fall of 2003, with my new confidence in studying, I entered Texas State Technical College (TSTC) in Waco, four hours from Galveston.

My studies included web software, web design, and computer programming. Web design caught my attention because it required creativity. Still, I also learned how to collect and analyze website usage to help improve social-media market performance, which I use successfully in several of my businesses.

Would I have my business successes without attending TSTC? I am not sure. But for sure, I would not have attended TSTC without first deciding to enroll.

Decisions always come first.

As my time at TSTC was moving along in late 2003, just after I turned nineteen, I set my sights on another opportunity. I applied to work as a marketing representative for the best-known company in Texas, Dell Computer Corporation. Michael Dell started Dell in 1984, the year I was born, while he was a student at the University of Texas. He turned a $,1000 investment into $73 million in sales in the first year of operation. In 1996, he located the company in the town of Round Rock, Texas, about twenty miles north of Austin. Not surprisingly, Round Rock is named after a round rock in one of its streams! Go figure.

Besides Dell's status and fame, I was impressed by how one individual could make such a positive difference in so many lives, hiring more than 150,000 people worldwide.

In deciding to break from my Galveston past, I was determined to associate with business success. Dell was a perfect choice, and the company paid its employees well. I was excited to prove that I could earn good money working a real job instead of selling drugs.

In addition, Round Rock had one of the lowest crime rates in the country, while Galveston had one of the highest. I was not going back.

So, while still at TSTC, I filled out an application, walked it in, and waited. And waited.

I got no response. So, I applied again a month later. Still no response. I submitted sixteen applications over six months and continued to wait.

In November 2003, after finally getting a job at Dell Home sales division in Waco, I met the woman who stole my heart, saved my life, and made me a happy father. She turned me into a better man than I would ever be on my own.

TSTC has apartment-style dorms, and I was desperate to escape the temptations there. I moved to a low-income housing complex a few miles away, and she was my next-door neighbor. She says she first noticed me when I was moving into my apartment. I mean, I guess I am hot; we covered that already! Anyway, I could not have picked a more perfect time to show off my tattoos while I was moving my furniture.

It worked, but we didn't really speak for the first few months I lived there. Just the occasional hello as I would come and go to and from work or school. One day, our neighbor, Sookie Sue (A nickname, of course) knocked on my door.

"What's up, Sookie," I asked.

She didn't pull any punches. "Lety wants to see your tattoos."

I laughed. "She has to show me hers first."

That led to our first conversation. She told me her name was Leticia, but I could call her Lety. We became friends right away. The college is surrounded by restaurants, shopping, museums, and movie theaters, so there were lots of places for us to have some clean fun. We hung out here and there, and over time, I started to like her a lot.

Soon I got scared because I had spent a lifetime making sure I never let anyone get too close to me, not close enough to hurt me anyway. So, I tried to push her away but realized quickly that I didn't want that. I had to be honest with myself. For the first time, I had met someone I wanted to get to know and who wanted to be with me.

Believe it or not, after just a month, I was in love and determined to have Lety and Zek, now my son, be a permanent part of my life. Well, that is how it played out in my head anyway. She was mine; she just didn't know it yet.

Within two months, she had learned so much about me and my Galveston history that she was willing to visit with me to meet my family. We went on a lot of road trips together and got to know each other as much as we could as fast as we could.

Just about that time, I finally received a call from a Dell corporate manager, but it was not the call I expected. This is how the conversation went:

"Mr. Hegmann," he started. "I am calling you because I see you have done really well in our Home Sales division in Waco."

"Yes, sir!" I said, expecting that the call was the one I had been waiting for those past six months, with a job offer at Dell Round Rock.

"I am sorry to disappoint you," he said.

My heart sank, but I was not about to give up. "Believe me; I can do this job."

"The position requires high-level sales experience," he replied. "Your time in that position isn't what we're looking for, but your numbers are very good."

I wasn't sure where he was going with this.

I couldn't tell him about my successful drug sales experience in Galveston and the amount of money I had earned on the streets. So, I said the next best thing I could think of.

"How can I get more experience if no one hires me to get the experience?"

"I am sorry," he said. "We prefer to have reps with experience."

I was anxious to prove to myself that I could succeed in legitimate work. I had come this far on my own motivation, and I felt this next move would take me to the next level. I was not about to give up on a phone call.

With desperation growing, I tried a new angle. "Hire me, and I'll be your top representative in three months. That's my promise to you. If I don't do it, you can fire me."

He laughed, but my offer connected with him.

**"Okay, you got the job.
However, I expect results, not promises."**

"You have a deal," I said.

"We will contact you in the next couple of weeks to arrange your start date."

A few days later, in January 2005, while visiting Galveston with Lety, my Dell manager called. They were ready for me to get started and would pay my moving expenses from Waco to Round Rock. I had five days to rush back to Waco and pack.

This must have given Lety a small taste of the adrenaline I tend to live on. I asked her to move with me just two months after we met. I was asking a lot. I was asking a single mother who had just gotten out of an abusive relationship to take a chance on a boy on his way to being a man and come with me. She was hesitant and initially said no. I was heartbroken! I guess something told her to take a chance because, almost seventeen years later, she is still with me!

From day one, I applied everything I knew under the supervision of the great Andre Artis, the man who gave me the opportunity. By the end of the first month, I was the manager's top business sales representative and never looked back. I was "Representative of the Quarter" for nine straight quarters.

I was now earning $12,000 per month and was on the fast track to becoming a productive, high-performing, law-abiding citizen.

I was hooked on achievement.

My Dell experience was like another positive college education. Working for Andre and then Lori, I learned to take customer service to a new level. I learned persistence, receiving as many as ten Nos before making sales as high as a half-million dollars each. My goals became my motivation. Fear, regret, and disappointment were no longer my mindset.

Andre and Lori eventually helped me move up to Dell's high-performing marketing called the Sharks Group, where I sharpened my sales skills to a whole new level.

By their example, I learned about the power of entrepreneurship. Developing and owning a successful business could get you the only true freedom—financial freedom. They not only talked the talk; they walked the walk. Their professional path to success was so like mine, and it inspired me. Andre attended Huston-Tillotson University, and excelled at sales and marketing, not only at Dell but at Oracle and Dropbox.

Andre eventually left Dell to open a successful chain of restaurants called Krab Kingz. They can be found in Austin, Pflugerville, Temple, and Killeen Texas.

I am not even sure he realizes I follow him or that he made such an impact on my life. He now owns several businesses, and I eat at one of his restaurants two or three times a month.

After Andre left Dell, I remained a little longer until I had about thirteen years' experience with the company. I did not have plans to quit until a new manager came on board with an attitude that turned me off. By then, the Galveston self-doubts had faded, and my business confidence had grown.

I watched how Andre had taken his sales and marketing experience and entrepreneurial skills into the business world to build an empire. His friendship and leadership left a lasting impression on me and influenced me to start thinking about building my own business.

This raises another point. I read once that your income will be the average of the five people who have the most influence on you. The company you keep most often will determine your success or failure in life.

Today, I am grateful for my Dell experience and the influence of people like Andre Artis. He is one of the five key people who influenced me most. Allen Harris is another one of those people for me. He was my manager for much of my time at Dell Home Sales Waco, and just like Andre, he was an essential part of my growth and success.

In my spare time, I used the Dell experience and the positive influence from friends like Andre, Lori, and Allen. I tried many businesses. A few did well, but many failed. It didn't matter. Each time, I dusted my ass off and took the lessons I learned into the next venture. I started businesses like a party rental service and a Mud Run company. It was hard work, but I got a taste of the potential income and independence.

People at Dell who knew about my sideline businesses made fun of me. Yes, they thought it was funny, watching me bust my ass at my companies while holding down a full-time job at Dell. One business that did well was renting out bounce houses for backyard birthday parties. Dell co-workers would jokingly call me the "the bouncy house dude." One year later, my bounce house rental business was bringing in $15,000 per month. That was more than my Dell salary. The business was so successful that I was able to sell it for a nice profit and immediately started another one.

The jokers at Dell were no longer laughing.

But they were not the reason I left Dell. Most people are comfortable with an 8-to-5 gig. That's okay for them and in general. But it just wasn't for me. People who succeed in business are a small minority. We stand out because we do what most people won't do. We work harder and smarter than most people. And that's why we have what most people don't have. Laughers and jokers are not doers. They are in the majority, and there are lots of them.

Dell had lots of jokers and laughers, but they never bothered me. What I wanted from life for my family and me was way too big for me to let them get in my way. My goals were way stronger than they were.

I decided to leave Dell after they hired a new manager for me to report to. Most of my coworkers thought I should have had the position, and it was one I was promised. With all my time, experience, hard work, and success at the company, I already knew the job and could have taken it on from day one. I tried my best to work with this new manager, but the breaking point came when I was asked to train him. I was still in my twenties, and maybe they thought I was too young to be a manager. But if that were the case, wouldn't that also make me too young to train a manager, my manager at that?

I didn't get their reasoning, but it didn't matter by then. I knew my value and abilities in business. Just like I had outgrown the drug and contraband business in Job Corps, I had outgrown my job at Dell. I no longer needed someone to give me a job. I no longer needed Dell, and they made it clear they didn't need me, so with the new manager breathing down my neck, I quit Dell.

Galveston was now behind me. Dell was a good experience and taught me priceless lessons, but it too was now behind me. I was ready for the next chapter in my struggle for success.

The best was yet to come.

My rock and my life, Lety: Was I in love? Yes! I was determined to have her and Zek, now my son, to be a permanent part of my life. Well, that is how it was playing out in my head at the time anyway. She was mine; she just didn't know it yet.

CHAPTER NINE

WHAT LETY MEANS TO ME

My story would be incomplete, and my life would be nothing without the best friend I've ever had. The mother of my beautiful girls. My partner. My best friend and my wife, Lety. Sometimes, I choke back tears when I realize how much her love for me and her support for my dreams made all the difference in my life and our lives.

My journey from the Galveston experience was not easy on either of us. She had so many opportunities to walk away. Looking back, I can only say she believed in me more than I believed in myself. From the time I met her, whenever I was in trouble, health-wise or otherwise, she was there to rescue my ass. She continues to save me. Recently, she nursed me back from near death.

One of my biggest challenges is figuring out what I did in life ever to deserve her attention and love. My past was nothing like hers. She comes from a big, loving family, where food, laughter, fun, and loyalty made up their days. She must have seen something in me. Her faith in me to this day is my most powerful motivation. I owe her more than I could ever repay in one lifetime. The love, appreciation, and encouragement I receive from her and her family (now my family) are beyond anything I experienced in my youth. Besides what I received from Nanny, family love was as rare as snow in Galveston.

As our friendship and romance grew, I told her more about my Galveston experience. I wanted her trust, so I shared everything. In return, she listened and gave me total acceptance. The fear that my past would stain the rest of my life began to fade.

My past would not change, but I could change its influence on my future.

Lety knew that Nanny's ashes had been found in a plastic bag along a roadside in Galveston. She also knew how much Nanny meant to me and how devasting an experience it was to learn that my father and his girl-friend discarded the ashes, the way he discarded his children.

Lety surprised me by purchasing a beautiful urn for the ashes. Her act of compassion and understanding brought me to tears. I rarely knew such kindness from family and friends in Galveston, so it made a powerful impression on me, even years later.

Lety also taught me another lesson. If you have the right people in your life, you will do more to please them than you would to please your-self. Lety and my girls do more to lift me to new achievements than my motivation. They give me more life and hope than I ever had in Galveston.

I always thought I could never appreciate and love Lety anymore than I already did, but after surviving the year 2021, especially in March, I now realize how much I love this beautiful woman. She saved my life. The end was so close that I did not have the strength to hold the phone in my hand. I had her call my lawyer and business partner to prepare things to pass along to my family.

When I see pictures of myself in the hospital bed, sixty pounds lighter than when I was admitted, with tubes everywhere, and having no memory of most of it, it's hard to believe that I survived.

Lety never left my side, and I believe her presence saved my life.

It all started when I went into the hospital in October 2020 for esoph-ageal surgery, which I thought would be a routine procedure to correct my severe acid reflux. In addition, my doctor uncovered a liver issue that needed special attention, especially with weight loss. Lety stepped in to manage my nutrition so my weight could drop under 200 pounds.

My in-laws, Tina and Joe Portillo, also made themselves available to provide me with all the emotional and physical support I needed during these trying months. They are like the parents I wished I had. Only parents who love you would drive from Waco to Round Rock in the middle of the night to bring you medicine.

Anyway, the surgery was rough. It was painful to eat. Painful to swallow. That was only the beginning. As if this was a conspiracy to test my ass, I caught COVID in January 2021. That was also rough. By March, the doctors realized that my first surgery was a failure and had to be repeated, meaning they first had to undo the November surgery. I was admitted on March 12th for the surgery. Thirty-six hours later, the doctors realized that they had mistakenly cut my bowel during the earlier surgery, which led to Sepsis—the body's extreme response to an infection. It triggers a chain reaction all over the body. There is more than a 50% chance it will be fatal if not treated within twenty-four hours and 90% if not caught within 48 hours. More than 200,000 patients die from Sepsis every year! And here I was in septic shock.

They rolled me into surgery twice in three days for emergency laparotomies, which involved opening me from chest to belly button each time. I'm sure it was rough, but I was unconscious most of the time and have no memory of it. One sure sign of what I went through is the long-ass scar stretching up and down my torso. When I see myself in the mirror or in pictures, I notice the scar is trying to fit in with all my tattoos.

Guess who was awake and at my side for the entire time? My rock and my life, Lety. She watched over me like a hawk and questioned the doctors at every turn. She was taking no chances. Their mistakes had almost cost me my life.

Now you see why I love this woman with all my heart. She was right next to me in the ICU, day in and day out, and never complained. She cleaned me; she changed me; she fed me; she cried for me, and she fought for my life harder than I did. She's the reason I came home to my kids because she made me fight for my life.

My business partner, Patrick Connell, and my amazing friends, family, and staff also stepped up to the plate and kept the business and my home going while the doctors and Lety struggled to keep me alive.

This was the second time that I thought I would die. I beat the odds twice, so I am taking nothing for granted. I realize how lucky I am to hold my wife, son, and girls or take them out to eat so they can drive me crazy, or even have my oldest daughter call just to annoy me. I am proud of my son, who works his ass off. I have countless amazing nieces and nephews who look to me for advice and help when they need it. From where I came from, I feel like the luckiest man on the planet to have a family and time to enjoy them.

And I want that feeling for you too!

I know I talk a lot about money, but don't let that fool you. The material shit I can buy today is cool, but nothing beats spending time with my family. I learned that back in Galveston, sitting with Nanny watching game shows and eating milk-butter toast. Despite all the shit I have been through, Nanny's loving and giving spirit is still with me.

Things can change in an instant, so I appreciate every minute I have with my family. After spending almost thirty days in the hospital, I look at the pictures of me lying in that bed every so often, so I never forget how lucky I am.

It also led me to do a lot of soul-searching. When I look at pictures of my new home, 5,000 square feet, six bedrooms, and a swimming pool on six acres, it reminds me how far I have come in such a short time—from dealing drugs on the streets of Galveston, dropping out of school in ninth grade, almost losing my life, getting my GED in Job Corps, going back to college, and starting many businesses, failing at many, succeeding at some.

What got me this far? Hard work and persistence, without handouts. Period! My Dell journey alone spells it out plainly. I submitted more than a dozen applications with no response. But I did not get discouraged. I kept applying with persistence until I got it. When I did get the job, I followed through and delivered for thirteen years.

I make no apologies for my success, but I also don't share it to brag. I hope it shows you how much more each of us can do with our lives. Yes, I have acquired material things through my success, but those don't matter as much as the memories built by sharing them with friends and family. My family and friends enjoy everything I have with me. My home, boat, cars, whatever. It's all about enjoying life with those you love, and that's why I work nonstop.

My financial success also allowed me to reclaim a small part of my best memories with Nanny. A few years ago, I returned to Galveston and bought her house. It needed some repairs, but I kept the original wooden floors that creaked when she would walk from the kitchen to serve me a plate of food.

I recently chartered a fishing boat in Galveston and took my son, friends, and co-writer, Dunbar DC Campbell, fishing for a weekend. We stayed at Nanny's house and had a great time. Dunbar was wide-eyed and asked me a hundred questions as we toured the house and yard that held so many of my childhood memories. He stayed in the room where Nanny and I would watch *The Price Is Right*.

I showed him where I used to hide drugs and Playboy magazines. In the little room where I would repair my old bicycles with salvaged parts, the small window still has paint from when I would test spray paint for my bikes.

I also took him on a tour of all the places we had talked about for a year. When we crossed 53rd Street and Avenue S, he suddenly pointed out the window.

"That's Corner Bar," he said.

We had talked about it so often that he knew exactly where it was. He asked me if I wanted to return there later for a drink. At first, I said yes, but the more I thought about it, the less I wanted to. He understood. Maybe I'll be ready the next time we visit Galveston.

Yes, I have come a long way from Galveston. But I say all this to remind everyone who reads this book that I could not have done a fraction of what I have experienced since then without the success to back it up. It's a success anyone can achieve. I hope I can inspire my business students, trainees, and associates to do more, so they can enrich their family and friend circles with great memories. You can do it too! You just must adjust your attitude and apply the right tools. I share the tools later in the book.

That also means drowning out the negativity that can cloud your mind. You already know all the negatives I had to deal with that led me to attempt suicide at age fifteen. I faced ridicule and discouragement on my entire journey. Just expect it, drown out the noise in your head, and move on. One day, the people who fed you negatives will wish they had what you have. Work your ass off today as others won't, so one day, you will have what others can't.

Success is the best revenge, all by itself. You don't have to do anything to your doubters. Don't let revenge be your motivator—that's negative motivation. Look for the things that lift you because those will give you the energy to succeed. It's a natural chemistry. If you have all the right tools that help others succeed, but you're still not where you want to be in life, then look for your reason, your motivation, and your why. As we all know, life sometimes comes at us fast with many obstacles. Your reason to succeed must be stronger than the shit life will throw at you. Even after you reach your goals, life will continue to test you.

Every experience—good, bad, or painful, taught me lessons I hope I can pass on to my business students, partners, and family. Seeing others using my business plan and advice to change their lives gives me more satisfaction than all the things I have.

The greatest joys of my life come from my family. They are my greatest motivation. Once you find your motivation, you will be able to power through all the roadblocks and negativity that life sends you. Those are all temporary tests to see how badly you really want it for yourself and your loved ones.

My every breathing moment is about my family and my business, and how to balance my business success to enrich their lives and happiness. I am so grateful for my wife. Not a day goes by that I don't want to do something special for her. She fills my soul like no one in my life ever did, and for that I am never satisfied with how much I can do for her.

I wish all of this for all of you.

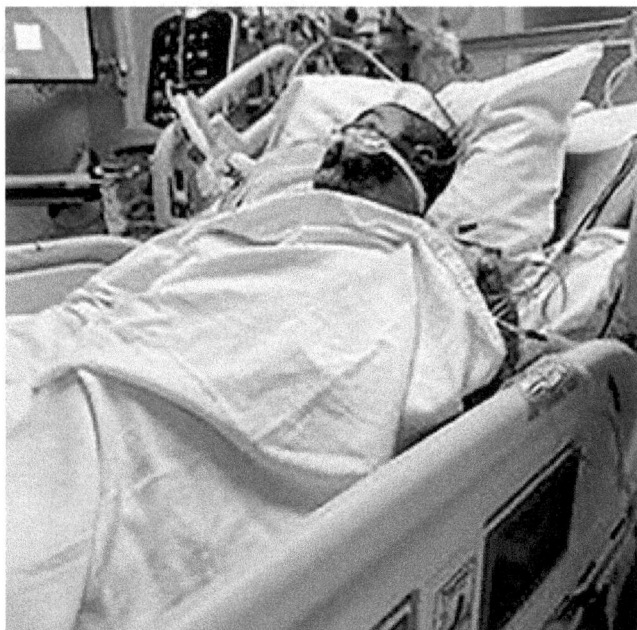

Close calls: Almost didn't make it (above), recovering (below). Learned a lot about delegation and family. Especially family. Without the love from Lety and the girls, I wouldn't be here today.

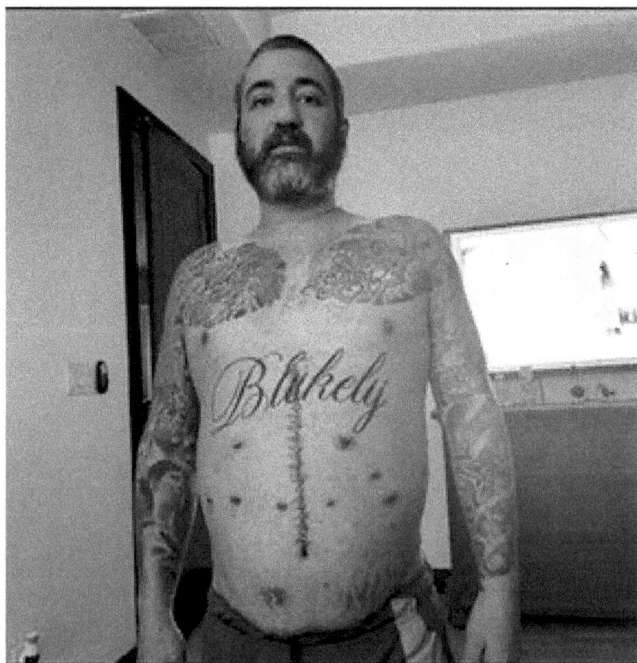

CHAPTER TEN

LETY TO THE RESCUE AGAIN!

After surviving months of COVID-19, surgery, and sepsis, another unexpected medical crisis popped up. Again, Lety was there to save my ass. She has never failed me in the seventeen years we've been together. This emergency was no exception. Before I share that experience, I should let you know that I was not lying on my back waiting for the doctors to give me a clean bill of health.

My doctors probably wished I had just stayed in bed. But no, we were living. Lety, my girls, and my nieces made sure I followed my doctors' orders as much as possible. I am not what you would call the easiest person to get to comply with instructions. My family is tougher on me than some of the doctors I had over the past year. Lety kept me on a strict diet and ensured I had minimal physical activities. One weekend when the boys and I headed to Galveston for a fishing trip, she called regularly to ask what I was eating. If I sneaked even a little potato chip, I had to get my fishing buddies to swear to secrecy about it.

When I take the girls out to eat without Lety, she checks the pictures. One day, she saw a picture on Facebook that the girls had taken the previous night when we went to a local restaurant. Lety had stayed home for a well-deserved night off.

The picture showed me at the restaurant table, laughing my ass off with the girls seated around me.

"What's that?" Lety asked.

"What's what?" I squinted at the picture, pretending I had no idea what she was talking about.

"That right there. On that plate."

"That's a salad."

"Not that plate, the one to the side." She pointed at a biscuit next to my salad.

"Oh, that plate."

She punched me on the shoulder. "You're driving me crazy."

"I know. I am good at it, right?"

"That's not what I mean! Look at the picture again."

"It's hard to see, and I don't remember. That was last night."

"Okay." She pulled her phone away. "Since you have problems remembering what you ate last night, no more restaurants this week."

End of conversation. No more restaurants for me that week.

Meanwhile, she was planning a great summer for us. One of the many reasons I love her so much. During all our challenges, she never forgets to keep me alive and living to the max. She always understood when I didn't want to do things because I always felt bad. These are things about her that I will more than make up for as we continue our lives together.

We don't have to go far to have fun with the family. I now have a home I could never have dreamed of as a kid. The backyard swimming pool, surrounded by manicured green lawns, is always the first choice for the girls, especially on those hot Texas days. I like hearing them splashing around and laughing even if I am not swimming. Plus, Lety is always planning the next meal on the grill that sits on the patio overlooking the pool. A huge leap from McDonald's dumpsters.

On lazy days, we just lay around the house watching TV and hanging out. And when the mood hits us, we head to the lake and cruise around on the boat, soaking up the sun and the good times. On clear nights, we sometimes sit around the fire pit in the yard, telling stories and laughing our asses off under the stars. If a few of my friends show up, Lety will let me enjoy a cigar with them or indulge in some good food.

In addition, I swear she trains those daughters she gave me to keep me on my toes. Take the youngest one, for example. At ten o'clock one night, while I was relaxing on the couch watching TV, she showed up in a swimsuit and long orange socks when she should have been in bed asleep.

She demanded I make her chocolate milk. I am no pushover, but when she looks at me all sad, I have no choice but to do what she wants.

Who else besides Lety would teach her to boss me around like that? Anyway, she got her chocolate milk.

Then, there's the middle one; she's nine years old. Some mornings, she puts on her roller skates and skates through the house, singing without a care in the world, happy as can be. I also recently got the girls a Playscape swing set and a playhouse, tube slide, and climbing wall. It keeps them outdoors doing physical stuff instead of always watching videos on their phones and playing iPad games. I try to balance how much I buy them with the time we spend together because their happiness is our happiness.

I will never forget my Galveston lessons.

I also never forget to spoil Lety every chance I get. For her birthday, I took her and some friends out for a nice dinner and drinks. I also bought her a lovely red purse because she likes red, and I wanted to get it for her. We enjoy doing things for each other and surprising each other every chance we get. I get a lot of pleasure from spoiling her whenever I can. She deserves it.

However, just leave it up to Lety to outdo all the fun we have at home. She put together one hellacious trip to the coast for Father's Day, making me wonder what I did to deserve her and the family I now have. She set us up on the 19th floor at South Padre Island's beautiful beachfront Sapphire Resort and Spa. Sitting on that oversized leather couch, breathing in the ocean air blowing through the open sliding doors, and looking straight out to the endless blue sea was priceless.

It was hard to leave the condo to go down to the beach. But once we got there, we had a lot of fun swimming in the clear waters and laying out in the sun with the family. It was easy to forget to keep checking my phone for messages or even answer it.

Of course, we had to eat at the finest restaurants in town. Friends recommended Daddy's Seafood and Cajun Kitchen in Port Isabel for the best seafood. For lunch one day, Lety got the biggest table, smack in the middle of the restaurant, for all nine of us—me, Lety, our daughters, and our nieces. I felt like a king surrounded by all these young ladies. Despite all I had been through, I felt like the luckiest man I know. We had fish, crab legs, shrimp, you name it. And no surprise, Lety pushed me to eat more mixed veggies and fewer potatoes.

Just like the advertisement for the resort said, the Father's Day vacation was a true getaway for the body, mind, and soul. I needed that, especially after the last year, and Lety knew that better than anyone else.

Back at home, the fun continued. Lety's family came over to celebrate two birthdays— her aunt and my daughter. We weren't able to get the whole family to join us, but there were enough of us to put on a great party. That was only the beginning. During the first week of July, we had friends and family coming and going every day. The days started early, ran all day, and ended as late as 2:00 a.m.

Mouth-watering aromas from the kitchen and the grill spread everywhere. We had races, cannonball contests, and water-soaker shootouts in the pool. We spent a lot of time drinking, bullshitting, and playing loud music. We had such a blast that we almost forgot to check our phones, which usually kept us occupied. It was a great time for all the cousins to get to know each other and bond. On July 4th, we had our own fireworks show to light up the sky.

It was a true family celebration I had been missing all my life—a celebration of life and financial freedom.

Lety had given me such an amazing summer; I was beginning to slowly forget all the medical shit I survived over the past year. I was ready to pour it on again and crank up my businesses to new levels.

In the meantime, I went in for what I thought was a routine heart scan. It surprised me when my Agatston score which shows the total area of calcium deposits and the density of the calcium in my coronary arteries came back very high. Since a high score may indicate an enhanced risk for a cardiac event, I was referred to a cardiologist, who ordered a Cardiac catheterization (also called cardiac cath), a procedure that shows the blood vessels around my heart. A long, narrow tube called a catheter was inserted into a blood vessel in my leg and guided all the way up to my heart. Then, contrast dye was injected into the blood vessel through the catheter to produce X-ray videos of my valves, coronary arteries, and heart chambers.

This cardiac cath showed that I had eight blockages ranging from fifty to ninety percent! As bad as those numbers were, I can only imagine how much worse they would have been if Lety was not watching every calorie I consumed. The doctor immediately recommended heart surgery, saying I had zero other options, not even for stents. A stent is a tiny, expandable metal mesh coil that is inserted into the artery to help keep it from narrowing or closing again. The stents are coated with medicine to prevent scar tissue from forming inside the stent, which could cause the blood vessel to become narrow again. Compared to open-heart surgery, stents are relatively safe, and very few people have complications from them. So, when the doctor told me stents were out of the question, he scared the hell out of me. His attitude was so cold that I decided to get other opinions. I am glad I did.

Two other doctors completely disagreed with his recommendation, saying I had typical blockages that could easily be stented, and at my age, the very *last* thing they would do is bypass surgery. The fact that these two doctors did not know each other and did not share each other's notes made me feel even more confident about their opinions.

My first doctor was full of shit. He was strictly in it for the money. The other two were salaried doctors who would have received the same salary, with or without surgery. This experience taught me that people have to stand up for themselves. Even professionals can have bad intentions or make mistakes. You must advocate for yourself. Always get a second opinion instead of accepting the first recommendation.

It's your life. Not theirs.

So here we go again, another medical procedure to save my life. I got stents in early September, with Lety anxiously counting the minutes in the waiting room. After a few hours of observation, I was sent home to recover with a long list of possible issues to watch for and activities to avoid, especially strenuous activities. I knew she would be watching everything I ate and did for the coming weeks. I got ready for my daily supervision like a kindergarten kid. At home, Lety became my principal, boss, nutritionist, doctor, and physical therapist—all with love. I am a lucky man!

The incision in my arm to get to the blood vessel had to heal before I could resume normal activities. In other words, no strenuous activities. Until my skin was fully healed, I would not be able to do things like swimming. It looked like I would be sitting on the patio watching everyone else enjoying the pool.

I wish they had been more specific about what strenuous activity meant. No one said I couldn't play with my kids in the living room. Three days after my stent procedure, I was roughhousing it with my girls. Lety kept an eye on us from the kitchen in case I overdid it. There was some pulling, tugging, and lots of laughter. Nothing unusual.

Well, I guess I did overdo it. I felt a little dizzy and thought it was just fatigue from playing. So, I sat quietly on the couch for a few moments. Lety had her radar on, took one look at me, and knew something was wrong. In no time, I was back in the hospital.

I had Atrial fibrillation or AFib. The doctors explained that it's like a quivering or irregular heartbeat that can cause all kinds of shit—blood clots, strokes, and heart failure. They said untreated AFib doubles the risk of heart-related deaths and increases the risk of stroke five times. They did say I was lucky because most people have no idea how risky it is. Now I do.

So here I was again, laid out on a hospital bed, with Lety at my side, holding my hand and telling me all kinds of things that made my heart rate go up in a good way. I tell you, she is a Godsend.

I can only think that all the ups and downs of the past year were for good reasons. To appreciate my wife and family more. To test my resolve to build my businesses so others could enjoy the level of success I was blessed with. All I could say at this point is, bring it on!

As you read this book, keep in mind that it was written during one of the most challenging years of my life. I had COVID-19, near-death experiences with multiple surgeries, sepsis, heart issues, and days in an unconscious state. Nevertheless, we kept writing. I spoke by phone or Messenger with my co-writer when I could. He would send me questions, and I would respond with more detail. Then he would write and send me chapters to review for accuracy and make edits. Back and forth for the past year. With all the challenges, we could have put the book on ice. However, that's not how you reach big goals in life.

Writing this book was also difficult because I had to dig up my past again and relive the Galveston days that had caused me so much emotional pain growing up.

My co-writer also wrote a book about his own troubled past, so he knew what to expect. I told him things about my early life that few people know. Some things will never show up in the book. He never over-whelmed me with questions, and he backed off when he knew there were things I did not want to talk about. He never pushed. He knew it was my story. I had to talk about it my way and on my terms.

He did tell me that writing my story would make the painful memories less painful. Some things are much easier to talk about today than a year ago. I look forward to the days when all or most of it will be easier to talk about. Until this book, the only person I trusted enough to talk about those early days was Lety. She always listened with patience, understanding, and love. She made it possible for me to write this book and gave me the confidence to overcome the fears I felt. The more I free the memories, the freer I feel. I love her even more for it.

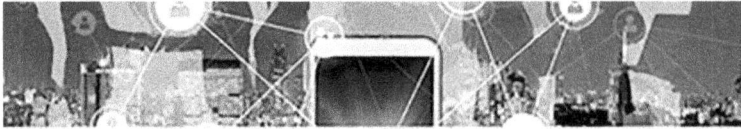

The Social Agent
Private group · 38.8K members

The Social Agent is a proven and fine-tuned wealth generating system for anyone seeking to become financially free through real estate. It's the reason other companies take our name. It has trained more than 48,000 students in 10 countries to generate an estimated $3 billion in total business.

View in Web Browser

WHAT'S NEW?

Complete system refresh for current subscribers:
Update to your current ads | New Seller Ad | New Wholesale Ad
New Subscribers receive:
Creation and Setup of all ads | New Seller Ad | New Wholesale Ad

Message me HERE and let's see what I can do for you!
Join The Social Agent Facebook Group to see reviews and results!

Don't forget to register for the upcoming Buyer/Seller Ad overview and Follow-Up Session!

Sign Up Here

CHAPTER ELEVEN

THE PATH FROM STRUGGLE TO SUCCESS

I started this book by saying this would be more than a story about struggle. Yes, the first part was about my early years of struggle, risk, pain, and disappointment. I also promised to show you the path I took to build success and make them available to you.

As I sit here on a Friday night, thinking about how I turned my life around, the ideas pour out on ways I can share my success plans with you.

My near-death experience in ICU a few months ago makes me even more motivated and focused on publishing this book and getting it in your hands. I am not writing this book to make money. I hope you apply the hard lessons I learned to enrich your personal and family life.

I also want to provide you with a valuable blueprint for your financial future so you can benefit from what I learned in my years of experience in real estate and other businesses. I want to put your business on the path to growth.

**This book is more than just "look what I have done."
This can be a success manual that can show you what
YOU can do.**

It is no bullshit. During the past five years, through *The Social Agent* program (named by my niece, Fallynn) I have trained more than 48,000 individuals in ten countries to generate almost six billion dollars in total commissions. This represents an average income of $150,000 per trainee for the leads my system generates.

At the current pace, that number is expected to be between eight and ten billion dollars by the end of 2022.

Yes, that's me. The same kid that dropped out of school just after finishing 9th grade to run the dangerous streets of Galveston.

The same kid that enrolled in Job Corps, *where bad kids go* to get a GED and an HVAC certificate.

Yes, that's me, the same kid. I was ridiculed so much by friends and family that I started believing I would amount to nothing.

This is the reason I don't accept excuses. People can change. Period.

It might sound repetitious, but that is my message in this book—making changes to your life. I also want to share the information with those who may not have $2,999 to invest in my program. This book is a journey from when I had nothing to where I am today, with seven businesses earning millions in sales each year. Make no mistake though, 2021 was a hard year personally and professionally. COVID took a toll on us personally and hit our bottom line. But it taught us that how you fight to recover is what matters.

When people say it takes money to earn money, they are dead wrong. It may require a few dollars to invest in yourself, but the true engine of success is the motivation inside you when it is applied to a proven plan.

The business plan I use in real estate will now be available in this book to both new trainees and all my loyal legacy clients. It is important that people read the entire book. All of it is meant to be brief and straightforward as possible.

The following section covers the formula that Patrick Connell and I have used to help tens of thousands of clients build wealth. It is what we studied, what we know, and what we applied to build our businesses. We hope it provides you a path to financial success as it has for thousands.

I got my early start in the Bounce House and Party Rental Business. I learned a lot about marketing, taxes, people, and contracts. I poured much of that experfience into the Social Agent. Now tens of thousands of real estate entrepreneurs around the world benefit each day.

CHAPTER TWELVE

HOW I VENTURED INTO BUSINESS

Getting into business didn't come as easy for me as some people looking in from the outside may think. However, I now know that I have been training for it my whole life without realizing it in the early years. In my mind, the drug trade is no different from any other business except that it's illegal. Well, at least back then, it wasn't any different to me. I understand now that what I was doing was wrong, but it was all I knew as a kid. I had to survive by any means.

I shared earlier that I had a hard life growing up. Selling drugs and illegal activities were a daily part of it. It was my reality, handed to me before I knew I had choices. Drugs or otherwise, lawlessness was all around me, on the streets, in the schools, in my home. My friends, enemies, mother, father, and just about everyone I knew were involved in one illegal activity or another. It was a way of life—the only way I knew until the day I almost lost it all.

That day changed my life forever. Something clicked inside me and I decided it was time to do the right thing. I had to find another way to live, not just survive. So, I gave up the drugs and applied to attend Job Corps. I learned a lot there: how to study, manage my time, and set goals. I earned my GED and entered college. Fast forward a few years and I was working for Dell Inc. (formerly Dell Computer Corporation) while still attending college full-time. I was on my way, and the change felt good.

Dell was the first real job I ever had, and I was determined to be the best employee in the company. I started in the Home Sales division, selling computers to people who saw our commercials and called us.

I quickly learned that I could apply the same knowledge
I'd used selling drugs to sell Dell computers.

It was simple. Same process, different product. I had to learn who my audience was and what they wanted. Everything from then on was easy. The best part was that I made good money without looking over my shoulder. Once I got a taste of legal achievement, I was hooked.

I was the Sales Representative of the Quarter for nine quarters in a row. That's when I knew sales was the right calling for me. I was good at it. After spending a little more than two years in that role, I was offered a position in the business department. After interviewing with them just days prior, Andre Artis and his co-manager Lori Nunez called me on New Year's Eve, 2005.

I recognized Andre's professional, straight-shooting, no-nonsense voice immediately. My heart raced knowing what this call could mean for the future I wanted for my new family.

"Happy New Year, Will," Andre started.

"Happy New Year to you both," I said, trying to keep my voice steady.

He wasted no time in jumping into the reason for the call. "Are you ready to come to Round Rock and be on my team?"

"Yes, sir!"

Within a few days of my offer, I left Waco to work at Dell's corporate office in Round Rock, Texas, about two hours away. I was in a new city with my now wife and son trying to figure out how to make this new life work while keeping up with the sharks in this company.

I immediately got to work applying the same formula to the business department that I used selling illegal drugs on the streets and marketing Dell computers to individual buyers. I had to learn the people, process, and product. Everything else just fell into place. By this time, I was still attending college remotely. I had no business knowledge other than working for the home sales department, and I was way out of my league, or so I thought.

I worked in the business queue for four years, and during that time, I took every opportunity to learn as much as I could from that company. Dell offered many training classes from technical to business subjects, and

I attended them all. While my coworkers were bothered about being required to attend these "boring trainings," I was intrigued. I took those opportunities to soak up as much information as possible, and it paid off big time.

At the end of my first year, I was yet again representative of the quarter and held that ranking for another two years straight. That eventually paved the way for me to move to the corporate accounts division, with the responsibility to generate and manage more than $10 million per year in business. That may not seem like a lot to you, but it was huge for me. I used the knowledge Dell gave me to outsell 99% of their marketing staff and create a life for my family that I could only dream about before. Each passing day that I succeeded at Dell was another day further away from my past in Galveston. The change felt great. Finally, I was doing what I was born to do, and I didn't have to break the law to do it.

I worked at Dell for more than twelve years. Every day, I am grateful that Dell took a chance on a young man with no prior experience. Dell boosted my confidence in myself so much that I decided to start my own business while still working there. From 2007 to 2012, I started many companies. I failed quite a few times along the way, but I always managed to pick myself up, learn from my mistakes, and try again. That's how I learned that people only fail if they fall and stay there. If you keep getting up, you're stronger and wiser each time.

By the time I was twenty-three-years-old, I started a party rental company renting moonwalks, waterslides, cotton candy machines, snow cone machines, etc. My co-workers often made fun of me for being the "moonwalk guy" or "the bouncy house dude."

I can only assume the reason was some people couldn't wrap their head around why one of the most successful reps in the company was delivering party rentals. I always had an unexplainable urge to do more. I know now that I am entrepreneurial at heart. It's in my DNA to strive to be better and to grow not just for myself but for my family. I was then, and am today looking forward to the next challenge, the next chance to learn, and the ability to grow to be a better businessman.

I sometimes wonder how many kids on the streets today are just like me, wanting to do more with their lives, but seeing illegal drugs as their only option. I hope this book will end up in their hands and help to change their paths. However, like me, they will likely face people who will try to put them down for doing something new.

By the end of my first year as the "the bouncy house dude," those who made fun of me would have been surprised to learn I was pulling in over $15k a month renting bounce houses for backyard birthday parties.

That was more than double my Dell income. I guess the joke was on them. Before I knew it, I had grown the business so quickly that I was receiving offers to buy me out. That's when I knew I had what it takes to build a great company and capitalize on it. I sold that business for quite a bit of money, and since I wasn't under a non-compete agreement, I launched a new one. I did this a few times until I decided to move on to a new venture.

Not every business I entered was good though. I had my issues, and I took my losses, and some of you will also. How you pick yourself up is all that matters.

Let me show you what failure looks like. It's not necessarily a bad thing. In fact, it taught me valuable lessons and allowed me to make mistakes that I was sure to never make again.

After selling my last party rental business, I started seeing ads on Facebook for these 5K fun runs that appealed to hard-core participants. For example, there were ads for mud runs, essentially an obstacle course with a lot of mud. Other variations included foam runs and bounce house runs. I thought to myself, *You know, you would be pretty good at this.*

I worked my ass off on a business plan for a mud run and found an investor to infuse us with $250k to get my new venture started. I was scared to do this myself, so I enlisted the help of a good friend and neighbor to go into business with me, with big hopes and dreams that it would work.

We started building out the systems and eventually locked up the venue for our first ever hardcore obstacle race out of Cedar Creek, Texas. We worked together day and night, marketing, securing locations, live music, big stage, staff, construction, the works! Within four months, we had 2500 participants and things were looking up—until they weren't.

Unfortunately, one of our participants was severely injured during this first and last event. To make matters more complicated, funds came up missing in the account and unexplained payments were made to entities outside of the business for personal expenses. It caused a rift between me and my partner at the time. To safeguard my investor, I returned his investment and walked away from that business.

Mismanaging the funds also led to serious tax issues and potential legal battles—more reasons why having a good CPA and attorney is essential.

I learned quickly that who you choose to do business with can make or break you. It quite literally means the difference between being profitable or being a complete failure.

NEVER give up too much control to any one person.

To date, I still consider that my biggest business failure and my biggest success. Why? Because it taught me a whole lot about what not to do in business.

For example, you must have a good bookkeeper, CPA, attorney, and people you can trust by your side. You can't just trust that people will do what they say and be honest in everything they do. When it comes to business, you must put friendship aside and put the business and its employees first. I vowed to never make that mistake again.

Fortunately, I was working for Dell during this, so I still had a steady income. However, toward the end of 2012, things at Dell started to turn sour. I was tired of being overlooked for positions I deserved. I wasn't the only one either. Many of my colleagues were passed over for managerial roles since they weren't friends with the right people. Politics had become more important than production. I'd given my all to this company, but one person kept holding me back. Some say it was because I was his best agent and he made a lot of money from my sales. Others thought it was because I wasn't a part of the club where people kissed ass for special treatment. I have never been and will never be that person. I got to where I am today by being strong, sticking to my guns, and seeing things through to the end.

The final straw came when someone with zero experience was hired for a managerial role over me and my team. I had the experience and qualifications to fill that position. After he became my boss, I was asked to train him to do the job. I decided I was done.

That day, I turned in my badge and walked away from corporate life. I was sure I would regret my decision, but it turned out to be the best decision I ever made.

**Sometimes, you must let some doors slam
in your face to see others you can open.**

I wanted to do my own thing and no longer pursue a corporate career. A former client I worked with for many years approached me and said, "I heard you left. You and I should talk about opening our tech shop," and Crossroads Technology Group was born. We went on to grow that company over the next two years venturing into healthcare, IT managed services, and sales. Starting that company challenged everything I had learned about business throughout the years. I was no longer an employee. I was the boss responsible for the livelihoods of others depending on my partner and me to make sure they had jobs.

I learned even more about myself while building Crossroads Technology Group. I realized just how important it is to have the right team around you. Eventually, we sold the company to a competitor.

It was a good business decision, but I was not able to negotiate a non-compete agreement as I had done with the bounce house business. The buyer wanted to ensure we wouldn't end up back in that space and take clients from them. I signed the offer, took my check, and walked away. It was time for me to find a new calling in a different industry, outside of tech, moonwalks, and 5K mud runs. I had no idea what I would do next. That's when my older sister said, "Why don't you just get your real estate license, dork?" And so it began. I started real estate school and received my license within nine months.

When I first became an agent, I was lost. I knew I wasn't cut out to be on a team because my mentality was always to be the boss and not someone else's errand boy. I did well, but it wasn't enough for me. I worked my ass off but couldn't get myself to a point where I felt like real estate was my final calling. I went back to what I knew best, creating a product that works and selling it. That's when *The Social Agent* was born. This proven method helps real estate agents expand their businesses and experience financial independence.

Business success requires the right partner (Patrick Connell, above) and a great team (below). I would not have accomplished any of this without them.

CHAPTER THIRTEEN

THE SOCIAL AGENT

Real estate was a brand-new world to me. I had no idea what I was doing or where to start. So, I did what every new agent seems to do: buying website leads instead of creating my own. I called my sphere (which I hated doing), badgered my friends, posted online even though no one cared, and spent thousands of dollars on dead-end lead generation companies promising the world and under-delivering every single time.

LEAD GENERATION

Then, I met my good friend Doug, a loan officer in Austin, Texas. He said, "Let's meet for coffee, and I'll show you how we generate leads and give them to our agent partners." So, we met, and I heard him out. Over the next few months, he and I shared marketing ideas from how to obtain buyers and sellers and everything in between to learning how to effectively generate our own leads for little money.

When I discovered Facebook lead generation, business started to take a massive turn for me. My tech background and marketing skills from Crossroads took over. I was obsessed with learning the ins and outs of Facebook, and I wasn't going to stop until I was the best at it.

I set out to learn every aspect of the platform and how ads work in the minds of the marketer and the end-user. I wanted to know everything about what makes an ad effective. After nearly a year, I figured it out, but it didn't come easy. Many nights I stayed up until 5 a.m. I strained my marriage and ignored my family as I worked nonstop.

Once I found a way to balance it all, I could excel in what I was doing. I started generating a ton of leads for myself and closing multiple deals from them. I was killing it!

Then, one night in 2016 I was online in one of the Facebook real estate groups, and a group member asked, "How do you all generate leads? Please help; I'm struggling." Little did I know that my answer to that question would write my future and become *The Social Agent*. I answered, "Here is how I do it."

Soon, I had agents beating down my door asking for help, and eventually, it turned into what you see today. So, what is *The Social Agent*? It began as a Facebook group that I could use to manage lead generation trainees and is now a string of multiple businesses under one umbrella.

When creating ads for any business, you must know all the moving parts. You can't just throw out some old run-of-the-mill basic ad content and expect it to be a success.

Listen closely because I usually charge more than two thousand dollars for this information in my training. I am giving it to you for free in this book. Once you understand your business and what you want to accomplish (i.e., generate leads for home buyers and sellers), then you can start creating ads to generate leads that find ready customers for your business.

Before creating an ad on any platform, you must know:

- Your market
- Your demographics
- Your target audience
- The style of graphics or videos that work best
- Verbiage to use to draw the users' attention
- Calls-to-actions to use
- How to automate the process so that prospects receive messages upon initial sign-up.

Let's talk about the market and demographics first. I am located in Austin, Texas, a very music and art-centered city, so I know my target market of 25- to 55-year-olds love music. I must appeal to these folks with my ads and make sure I can catch their eye by using loud, colorful, and compelling photos or videos to draw attention.

Other cities like Dallas for example, have very business-focused, nine-to-five professionals who prefer a cleaner look to their ads. That is what the data suggests at least.

Make sure that you fit your creative ability to your area. Focus on who you plan to target. In my area, I'm targeting the folks who are buying and selling homes the most, so it makes sense to focus my advertising budget on those individuals. Targeting involves more than just an age group, though. You must know what your prospective clients are doing online or what they are searching for to get to the right folks.

Some basic targeting tools I use are Zillow, Realtor.com, Homes.com, and Real Estate as interest targeting. Meaning folks who like those pages or pages related to those topics will be targeted in my ads. That gives me the best chance of getting my ad(s) in front of the right people who are currently searching for what I can offer.

CREATING ADS

Now that we've figured out our market, demographic, target audience, and creative (graphics), we need to use the correct verbiage. We want these people to engage with you. You must let them know, "I have what you want, and to get it, you need to pay attention to my ad."

Here is an example of my verbiage on an ad for someone looking for reduced-price homes.

(TEXT BODY)

ATTENTION (CITY NAME) & ALL SURROUNDING AREAS!!!!!

Don't waste time driving around or searching websites for hours! I have compiled a list of all price-reduced homes to be sent out to you weekly. Completely free for anyone in our area!

(HEADLINE)

CLICK "LEARN MORE" TO ACCESS OUR LIST OF ALL PRICE-REDUCED HOMES
(LINK DESCRIPTION)
Can you afford to miss what's on this list?
(CALL TO ACTION BUTTON)
LEARN MORE

I structure the ads this way for a reason. In the headline "ATTENTION CITY NAME," I am letting them know this ad is for their area. Then, I identify their problem! I know these people have been searching for homes online because I have targeted those folks with my interest targeting. So, I put *"Don't waste time driving around or searching websites for hours!"* In doing so, I just identified a problem or frustration.

Next, I want to give them a solution to their problem, so I use "I have compiled a list of all price-reduced homes to be sent out weekly. Completely free for anyone in our area!"

I have now offered them a solution to their problem, and I tell them how to access the solution by putting *"CLICK LEARN MORE TO ACCESS OUR LIST OF ALL PRICE-REDUCED HOMES."*

Next, I want to bring it home by making them feel like they will miss out by not taking advantage of my offer.

"Can you afford to miss what's on this list?"

When prospects read this, they feel like they will miss an opportunity by not clicking and submitting their information.

Finally, I put the *LEARN MORE* button at the bottom so potential clients can click, enter their information, and submit it to me.

At that point, the information is sent to my Customer Relations Management (CRM) system and an automatic text and email response is sent to the prospect. I also include specialty information that I teach in my training. For more in-depth information on that, feel free to check *The Social Agent* for help at any time!

See what I did there? I identified a problem YOU have and gave you the way to fix it by suggesting you join my group and get the information you need there. It's the same thing I explained above but with a different product.

Now, you have a step-by-step formula to create effective ads!

Throughout my career with *The Social Agent*, I have met tens of thousands of amazing people. One of whom trained with me and became my business partner in multiple other ventures. (More on this in the next chapter.)

To reiterate, I trained more than 48,000 agents, in many countries such as the USA, China, Germany, New Zealand, Australia, and others. My trainees collectively generated more than $7 billion dollars in commissions (and that's just the data I know about) which average about $150,000 in commission per agent since we started the training program.

Any system you put work into will work for you if you work it, remain steady, and always look for ways to improve and strive to be the best.

That said, I will end with this: It doesn't matter how well your product works, how much money you make with it, what you do with it or how you run your company on the back end if your customer service and follow-up is poor, you will fail. I built *The Social Agent* so I could offer a great product and great customer service. You can probably attest to that. If you aren't a trainee, all you have to do is check *The Social Agent* group and see the thousands of reviews in there for yourself!

Remember the trainee-turned-business-partner I mentioned? His name is Patrick Connell. Meeting him was one of the best things that could've happened. His family is like my family and vice versa, and we have built some amazing businesses together, which is why I noted the importance of aligning yourself with the right people. We will talk more about that in later chapters.

Please don't tell Patrick I said any of those nice things about him. If he asks, tell him I said that meeting him was the worst thing ever!

Social Agent University was founded by William Hegmann and Patrick Connell, as a way to help as many agents as possible take advantage of solid, useful information to grow and run their businesses. Using their business, social media, and real estate backgrounds, Social Agent University is sure to extend their reach to agents and brokers around the world.

William Hegmann, President

After 15 years in Technology and Sales (including 12 years at Dell Computers), William Hegmann decided to bring his technological expertise and sales experience to the Real Estate world. Since 2016, William has trained well over 16,000 real estate agents across the world (including the US, Canada, New Zealand, and South Africa) to generate leads using social media. To date, the Social Agent program has helped agents and lenders generate approximately 15 Million leads and facilitated over $10 million in agent to agent referral business.

On top of that, William co-founded Realty Solutions, a residential real estate brokerage based out of Austin, TX, and Lead Source Management, a lead generation, management, and follow-up service that specializes in

It's been quite a journey from the streets of Galveston. But the best is yet to come.

CHAPTER FOURTEEN

SISTER COMPANIES AND STRUCTURING YOUR BUSINESS

Now that you know the story of *The Social Agent*, I can take you to where we are now. *The Social Agent* was the first of what is now multiple businesses in multiple areas of the industry with multiple streams of revenue. We were able to do this without sacrificing our product effectiveness or customer service goals.

Shortly after meeting Patrick in 2017, we became friends. We talked about how we not only wanted to be in the industry, but we also wanted to try to change it. Eventually, *Realty Solutions*, our first business built off the backbone of *The Social Agent*, was born!

We worked hard and grew it smart. With a small investment, we promoted ourselves with a product not many brokerages were offering at the time: $495 per transaction and the agent keeps the rest. That product allowed us to grow fast and steady. Promoting our brokerage not only spurred growth but also boosted morale. Why? Because now *The Social Agent* wasn't just a marketing company. It became a brokerage that also teaches agents to market.

Who better to learn from than people who are in the trenches with you?

We grew fast and steady until COVID hit. Over the last twelve months, it's been slow but steady growth. After all this, we decided we needed to do more, so we set to teach agents how to generate and manage leads and offered to do it for them. We became a full-service, end-to-end, lead generation, and follow-up company. That's when *Social Agent Broker*

Edition was born! For a small monthly fee, our clients receive full service with an excellent closing ratio.

Again, another idea was born from what we had already been doing. We realized we needed to offer the training and ad set-up along with content for users to use, build ads, and stay up to date. So, in 2020 we created an online course called Social Agent University that drips out new ads, photos, data, content, marketing materials, etc., every week. We offered it as a monthly subscription or a lifetime membership for a one-time small fee. Some may think our success came from being in the right place at the right time, but it came from hard work.

We sold more than $1 million in net profits in the first seventy-two hours of launching that platform. I knew I had a large real estate industry following, but I didn't really realize it was quite that large. We had more than just a few companies; we had a large network of people all over the US and Canada looking for help with growth, while in turn, helping them change their businesses for the better. It was a win/win.

Once we had that membership practically running itself, we developed *Social Agent Network* to bring all our products from many sites to one big platform. Consolidating them made it easier for us to manage and more convenient for our end users.

One of the biggest issues agents have besides lead generation and content is which CRM to use. Are they following up with clients like they could be? Are they spending too much time doing it manually? We promoted many CRMs but none had everything we thought they should.

So, one day I said to Patrick:

"We need to develop our own CRM."

He looked at me in shock. "Are you crazy?"

"I believe we can do it."

"You're talking about paying hundreds of thousands just in development."

I insisted. "Let's give it our best."

That said, we did just that and developed a CRM that included all the features we believe agents want and need. Eventually, we launched what is now known as Social CRM Pro. The best part is we aren't overcharging. It is only $19 per month and includes a TON of features. Check it out for yourself.

Finally, we determined that too much of our business was based on digital sales. It isn't a bad thing, but companies need to be diverse so that the revenue won't dry up if the market shifts due to changing consumer demand. By 2021, we realized we had to be in other areas of the real estate industry. Flipping and wholesale deals came to mind, and with the help of my amazing team (yes, I'm going to name them here: Jen Walters, Luis Garibay, Khrystiana Valadez, Glenna Machado, and Ian Williams), we created and launched Home Offers Made Easy.

And in 2022, we launched Dash Construction Services to provide complete home renovations, remodeling, and roofing services.

Our process isn't perfect, but we learned hard lessons that you don't have to experience if you pay attention to what I said above and what I tell you in the following chapters. I will detail how we created these companies and leveraged partnerships and relationships to help us grow our businesses and our partner's businesses.

STRUCTURING YOUR BUSINESS

Properly structuring your business is essential for running a company effectively. Failure to do so could cause you to end up paying additional thousands or tens of thousands in taxes. I learned this lesson the hard way throughout the years. I own many companies and thought structuring them under a sole proprietorship was the best strategy.

Truthfully, it was just the easiest way, so I went with it because I had no idea how to set up all of this stuff myself. It wasn't until I learned how to trust others a little that this changed. I hired a CPA firm at the recommendation of my business partner, after receiving a $65,000 back-tax notice from the IRS. Before this, my taxes were a mess, and the "bookkeeper" or so he liked to call himself, was to blame.

The CPA firm reviewed my books for the previous four years, and I can't believe what they found. I was four years behind on payroll filings; my S Corp was not set up properly, and my taxes hadn't been paid on time. I was screwed. This was all a product of a novice businessman who didn't want to listen to others. It almost cost me big time.

In addition, my bookkeeper had done almost nothing for my Texas books. He just fluffed a bunch of numbers and plugged them in. Thankfully, I only ended up owing the IRS about $20,000, but that was offset by an income tax refund of about $17,000. So, I only had to pay about $3,000 to the IRS and $2,000 in fees to my CPA. That $5,000 potentially saved me $65,000 in potential IRS debt, and I have been with that firm ever since.

Most CPAs can help you save money, and many also offer services to set up your IRS EINs, business LLC, and S-Corp election. I opted to have my CPA do all this for me, saving me tens of thousands of dollars on tax payments each year.

Having a good CPA is only half the battle. I also recommend having a trustworthy attorney on hand.

I know this all sounds expensive, but I assure you these professionals pay for themselves and then some. So many things can go wrong in your business at any time, and having the proper combination of CPA and attorney is priceless.

Another example is the one I shared previously about the mud run, which led to a broken friendship, mismanaged funds, legal issues, and avoidable tax liabilities.

Before starting any business, big or small, please ensure your business is structured properly.

The goal of this book is to share how I started in business and all the wrong turns I made, so you can be ready before you have a chance to make the same mistakes!

Patrick Connell, Dean of Students

After 12 years as a Paramedic, Patrick Connell shifted gears completely and went into real estate. Having grown up inside of a real estate family, he hit the ground running and quickly grew a large client and referral database.

In 2017, Patrick, along with William, founded Realty Solutions, a residential real estate brokerage based out of Austin, TX. As the Broker of Realty Solutions, Patrick oversees the management of the office staff, compliance, and over 70 real estate agents. In addition to overseeing Realty Solutions, Patrick also teaches a variety of continuing education and legal update courses throughout Texas. In 2019, Patrick and William started Lead Source Management, a lead generation, management, and follow up service that specializes in helping real estate brokerages leverage lead generation for their agents.

In his spare time, Patrick loves spending time with his family, investing, reading, and learning as much as he can about a variety of topics.

My trusted friend and business partner. We have created opportunities for many, but this is just the beginning!

CHAPTER FIFTEEN

REINVESTING IN YOURSELF AND LEVERAGING PARTNERSHIPS

One of the hardest things I had to do for my business was to stop hoarding every penny I made in profit. Sounds weird, right? Hear me out. As an entrepreneur, you are always looking for your next paycheck and wondering where it will come from. It doesn't matter if you make $1 million per year; that feeling never goes away, and that is what drives a good businessperson to keep growing their business.

When I started in the business world, I was terrified to spend money on anything. I had a hard time accepting the idea of "You have to spend money to make money," so I spent as little as possible and tried to make it work. That was a huge mistake that I made more than once. I quickly learned after two failed businesses that my failures weren't due to a lack of drive or work but lack of opportunity.

What creates opportunity? Leads! What creates leads? Marketing! What do you need to market yourself to the masses? Money! While the above may not apply to everyone, it does apply to most of us running our own businesses. If you don't spend money getting your name out, you will fail. No one knows who you are if you don't get out there and tell them. Sure, we can make a Facebook business page and post our business on our timelines, Instagram, and the like. However, that doesn't do much.

Once I began running ads on Facebook and Instagram, I started getting real business in the door. You don't have to go all out at first either. You can start slow, spending $5 per day on ads if you can afford it to seed your brand awareness. In my business, leads are the most important, so I run lead ads and funnels to drive people to my Facebook group, where most of my business is generated. You need to identify what type of ad to run (I can help you with that if you take my training), stick with it long-term, and let the results flow. Again, most of us who fail to do this fail in business altogether.

REINVESTING IN YOURSELF

Once you gain a few clients, take 10% of that profit, reinvest it into your marketing campaigns, and increase your spending from $5 to $7 per day. Keep increasing your spend incrementally until your reach gets bigger and bigger. Your brand will start to be seen all over the place repeatedly to your target prospect.

Repetition is the key; prospects will start to recognize you and your business, and eventually, you will have business coming in from all angles.

Once I got my first few clients, I delivered an excellent service to them. Then, in addition to having business coming in from my ads and my Facebook group, but also referrals. Today, five years later, referrals make up about 60% of my business. Some people get comfortable after their business grows or become complacent. That is the quickest way to see your business go from something to nothing. Never stop marketing yourself! Old clients will eventually forget you, and you will always need new ones. Referrals are great, but they dry up if you don't have fresh leads to work, help, and get referrals. You never want to turn off the cycle. I have trained more than 40,000 people between the USA and Canada. Today, 40% come from my ads, and 60% are from referrals.

In March 2021, I got sick and was in the hospital for a month and out of the office for the following seven months. I thought it would be okay if I didn't market for new business. Really, in my case, I had no choice because I couldn't work anyway. Since I didn't have the right processes or people in place to help me, my business went cold. I went from training hundreds of people each week to struggling to get business once I got back in the game.

> Simply put, people weren't seeing me and forgot about me. Out of sight, out of mind. I had to fight to build my presence in the business again.

Do not make the same mistake. Always make sure you are marketing and plan for something bad to happen. The hope is that you never need to activate that backup plan. Not having such a plan almost killed the seven-figure business that I worked extremely hard to build. Thank God I had other team members to pick up my slack. However, I failed to train them on what I do, which had a lot to do with the fact that I was scared and refused to delegate tasks. I remember reading once that as a businessperson, *you must learn to delegate, or you will stagnate*!

I felt that if I gave up too much control, my business wouldn't be the same, so I worked myself to the bone, did most of the client-facing work by myself, and failed to train my team on how to do these activities. That really hurt me when I got sick.

Reinvesting in myself helped me grow from a few thousand to a seven-figure company within three years. Today, we run seven companies, using profits from each to help grow the next. Reinvesting in yourself is one of the most important things you can do. Never forget that.

LEVERAGING PARTNERSHIPS

Now that we've covered that, let's talk about leveraging partnerships. This is equally as important as reinvesting in yourself. It never hurts to have partnerships with people who also see your value and may invest in you too.

When I first started *The Social Agent*, I had a small following, but as we grew and became well-known in the real estate world, that quickly changed. Companies and individuals who wanted to either work side-by-side with me or sell their product in my group started to approach me. Learning which ones to choose was hard, and we made some wrong choices. However, we chose the right ones often and leveraged those relationships to help not only their companies grow, but ours as well.

In the beginning, I did one thing and one thing only. I helped people set up ads on Facebook and Instagram, while teaching them how to do it themselves. The results were phenomenal and allowed me to grow to over 48,000 trainees in five years. Along the way though, I realized there was a need for much more than just leads. Those same people needed to learn how to follow up, call prospects, have a user-friendly CRM, and the ability to delegate work to an *Inside Sales Agent* (ISA), etc.

I then started using a popular CRM platform, building drip campaigns and follow-up systems to use after completing my training. I referred thousands of people to them, and it was a win-win-win. I made money on referrals, they gained new user accounts, and my clients now had a follow-up system in place.

That part was only one piece to the puzzle though. Most agents need more than just a simple follow-up system that will text and email clients. What happens when those potential clients respond? Who will return their calls? Questions like these come up often. What if I'm out of town? What if I'm in a meeting? What if I'm at a showing? You can't be everywhere at once, and when working with new leads, speed is key.

If you aren't quick to respond to a hot lead, they will find someone who is. So, we partnered with a company that has mastered follow-up by receiving the lead from a source like Zapier and immediately texting the lead. The system is automated, but the texts look as if they are coming directly from you. If a lead responds, then a representative based in the U.S. picks up the conversation and gets as much information as they can before setting up a call for you to chat with the lead.

That system works very well, and it helped my clients make a lot of money over the years. It really is a pick-your-poison situation as there are many ways to go after leads. You can use email, text, virtual assistants, and Internal Sales Agents (ISA). An ISA is responsible for qualifying incoming leads, prospecting for new leads, and following up with past leads.

You must have a proper follow-up plan and system in place to track leads or you will fail.

Finally, we partnered with a company that conducts calls on behalf of the agent to gather information and set up appointments for the leads. You can choose to work with overseas ISAs or local US-based ISAs. The difference in price is about $4 per hour vs. $15-$20 per hour. I prefer the latter. These days however, calling is becoming obsolete, and many people don't answer their phones or return calls. Texting seems to be the best choice, but options for a cold call ISA exist and, in some cases, works very well.

All these relationships led us to where we are now. We offer our own CRM software, so we don't have to rely on other companies to help us. Social CRM Pro is the result of a lot of hard work to get this built for people to use in any industry, although it is mainly used by real estate agents. The system everything you could possibly need from a CRM provider. We learned a lot of lessons along the way that helped us figure out exactly what we were missing and what we needed to make it happen.

The only thing we haven't conquered yet is our own follow-up ISA service, which may not be too far down the road. However, for now, we are focusing on our trainees and CRM clients to help them grow as far and as wide as we can.

So, keep investing in yourself and leveraging the right partnerships. For you, that may be a lender who is willing to help pay for some of your marketing costs or a title company that is willing to help you send out mailers. Whatever it is, start it, stick with it, and kill that shit!

The faces and smiles that motivate me to do more each day. Lety, Jailen, Adyson, Kendall, Blake, Krystiana, Zek, Fallynn, Kaylan, Lilia, Aalyssiah, all of my nieces and nephews, and my in-laws. I love you all!

CHAPTER SIXTEEN

THE IMPORTANCE OF HAVING SUPPORT

When I started my business, I was all in and didn't need or want help from anyone. Or so I thought!

As a business owner, it is often hard to relinquish control of tasks to employees or even business partners. I struggled with delegating for the last five years, and it almost cost me my life. I worked myself to the bone from 2016 to 2020 when I was diagnosed with Gastro-Esophageal Reflux Disease (GERD).

Some people who have GERD experience it as more of a mild annoyance, and others see it as a disease that, if not fixed, makes you not want to live anymore. Sadly, I was in the latter category, and it was the beginning of a very rough road ahead.

When I received my GERD diagnosis in March 2020, I had only mild symptoms at that point. As the months went on, the burning sensations in my throat and chest were happening more frequently. Unfortunately, they soon became unbearable, and something had to change.

I visited doctor after doctor. Some of them believed me, and some did not. Finally, I found a surgeon willing to listen. Fast forward seven months and ten-plus tests later, I was finally approved for anti-reflux surgery.

Sadly, after all that time and money, the surgery was a failure.

My business was suffering because even though I knew I needed help, I refused to give up control and kept trying to do everything myself.

I couldn't give one hundred percent of my attention to my business activities because I was miserable all day, so things slowed down over time.

REINVESTING IN YOURSELF AND LEVERAGING PARTNERSHIPS

I finally hired someone to help take over my marketing business and do the work I needed while I was out. With their help and the help of my team, we kept our projects alive for a while, but business continued to slow.

I waited too long to ask for help, and it cost me hundreds of thousands of dollars in lost revenue.

I am not telling you this as a sob story. I am telling you this because I do not want to see this happen to anyone else.

Finally, I was able to get my surgery reversed and had a more traditional reflux surgery. Unfortunately, there were some serious complications that almost spun out of control. I spent a month in ICU and almost died. Again, my personal and professional life suffered because I wasn't taking care of myself.

Becoming ill with GERD and having no continuity or alternative plans in place damn near ruined my business. Doing everything yourself and not delegating tasks to others is a bad idea, for your business and your health.

Pace yourself and have the proper resources in place to help you when you need it.

Learn from my lessons, and don't let the same thing happen to you.

Having family support or another support system is essential. Sure, some people can do this on their own. I lived most of my life alone. I had "family," but none were truly there for me, especially when I needed them the most.

In Chapters Nine and Ten, I explained how Lety and my new family came to my rescue to give me all the reasons I needed to take better care of my health and my business.

I hope for your sake, that you find the same purpose and strength in your family.

Before and After. You have read and seen the amazing changes in my life. But this is not about what I have done. This is about what YOU can do with hard work, the right attidute, the right system, and the right people around you. YOU can do it too!

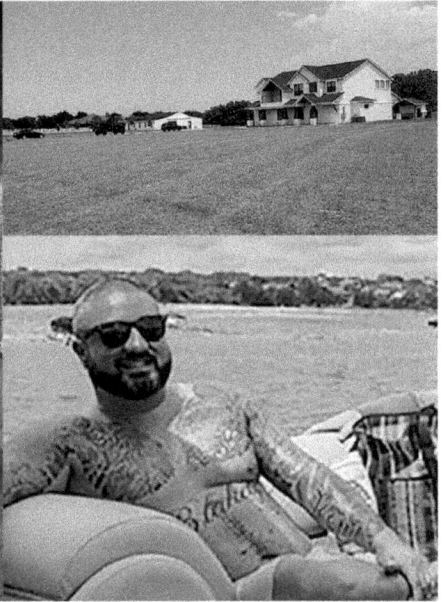

CHAPTER SEVENTEEN

THE FORMULA

By now, you have a pretty good idea of who I am and where I come from. I have shared stories in this book that some of my family members don't know (or didn't know until reading this). Now we're going to finish this book by talking about the formula. Well, it's more of a process, or my process anyway.

So, let's walk step-by-step through how I built my businesses. I believe you will succeed if you follow the same process. Remember, our products don't have to be the same, but the processes should be.

THE FORMULA – STEP-BY-STEP

First, you must know your product or service inside and out; make sure it works and you know what you are doing. I sell a service—training and an advertising setup process for Facebook (FB) and Instagram (IG). I have refined it to a point where it works so well that it sells itself.

Second, master every aspect of the product or service you are selling. If it's a house, make sure you know everything there is to know about houses. If it is a product or service, ensure there are not many similar or better alternatives available. You should know how to use that product or service better than anyone else. Also, you must be confident in what you offer so others will be confident in you and your product.

Finally, know that customer service is just as, if not more, important than knowing your product and its efficacy.

I have built all my businesses through customer service, and at least sixty percent of my new business comes from referrals or is based on reviews.

That is a significant amount, which means I am doing my job well.

When I started *The Social Agent*, I personally trained thousands of agents one-on-one and developed personal connections with each one of them. I understand not everyone can do that, and it did take a toll on my overall health. You can accomplish it by hiring the right people, paying your employees well, and ensuring they maintain the same level of service that you provide to your clients. I can assure you that an unhappy client can cost you a lot more than the time it would have taken you to fix their problem and change their experience with you from bad to good.

Sometimes, I help existing clients with small problems at no charge. In return, I get a great review that typically drives five to ten more sales to my door, which is $10-20K in new revenue, and the cycle repeats every week. I could charge a nominal fee for my time, but I probably wouldn't get a review. Plus, I will probably get referrals from those new clients.

Do you see how this works? It's simple! Be nice, be courteous, offer a great product or service, and provide great customer service, and your business will thrive as a result.

TARGET AUDIENCE

Not knowing your audience can set you back or even kill your momentum before it starts. Most products or services are not one-size-fits-all, and most business owners mistakenly believe that just getting eyeballs on the product is all they need. Actually, you must have the right eyeballs on it. If the product is for real estate agents and you are advertising to people in the car industry, you will likely fail to generate any interest.

Advertising must be precisely targeted. For example, on Facebook, I am allowed to target people by their interests. So, when I want to push my training out to agents, I choose professionals and anyone in the real estate industry. If I am advertising to homeowners or potential home buyers, I target folks with an interest in housing-related topics. Don't make it more complicated than it needs to be when it really is that simple. Creating ads, however, requires specialized training. I recommend you start by joining *The Social Agent* Facebook group.

SALES FUNNELS

The audience is only one piece of a multi-layered puzzle. You must also have a sales funnel. So, what is a funnel? For some, it could be a website or a landing page with a form for prospects to submit their information and generate a lead. My Facebook group is my funnel, and all my advertising routes agents into the group; I let the group do the talking for me. In my group, I have thousands of reviews and tons of proven data that intrigues the average user enough to reach out to me for more information on my services. That is how I get my leads, but you may get yours from Facebook forms, landing pages, or your website. No matter what you are doing, ensure you have a sales funnel set up for your business.

Once your funnel is set up, determine how to get your target audience to see and react to it. We create ads and route potential clients to either a Facebook form, landing page, or website by using paid Facebook and Instagram ads through Facebook's ads manager. We also set up the verbiage, ads, graphics, funnel, form, landing page, website, etc. for our clients who don't want to do it themselves.

You could always try the organic route, but that could take a hell of a long time before you get any substantial reach from the ad. That is probably not a risk you want to take because you may fail before you have a chance to succeed.

If you don't use Facebook to advertise, you can use YouTube, Google AdWords, or something similar. My point is you must use an advertising system or you greatly reduce your chances of success. Some may say, "Well, I can work in my sphere of influence." Sure, you can work your sphere of influence (SOI), with the risk of annoying your friends and family by bombarding them with your advertising. I assure you that everyone's SOI runs dry eventually, putting them back to square one, looking for ad platforms to advertise on. I heard this a long time ago, and it always stuck with me:

"A business without a sign is a sign of no business."

I believe that wholeheartedly.

REINVEST IN YOUR BUSINESS

Of course, you must first some money before you can reinvest in yourself, but once you do, you are golden. To obtain new business, I set aside ten percent of my net profits for marketing each month. Sometimes, I don't have to use it all, but I leave it there in case I need to use it for new advertising or as an "uh oh" fund if something random and costly pops up. Always remember this part of the book. I am going to repeat this one more time. Always set aside ten percent of your net profits (if you can afford it) for marketing or to use as an "uh oh" fund. Net profits are what you have left after paying all expenses, including taxes. Never make the mistake of not setting aside enough money to pay your taxes.

STRUCTURE YOUR BUSINESS PROPERLY

Properly structuring your business allows you to maximize your tax benefits and avoid paying more in taxes than legally required. Most agents will operate as a sole proprietor not realizing they will pay significantly more taxes than if they operated as an actual business.

My business is set up as an LLC with an IRS S-Corp election. I paid my CPA to set this up for me, which has saved me tens of thousands of dollars. Operating as a sole proprietor doesn't give you all the benefits that a corporation does. Also, by setting it up this way and paying yourself a salary, you are paying your taxes quarterly, avoiding possible default. I see so many agents and business owners who pay tens of thousands more in taxes than they should and still have a $50k -$100k IRS bill at the end of the year that they can't pay. I am just going to be blunt here and tell you what I tell my agents. DON'T BE STUPID. Pay a CPA to set it up properly to save yourself time, money, and heartache.

REMOVE NEGATIVE INFLUENCES

I had to learn this the hard way, and then I found folks who had the same ambitions as myself. Surrounding yourself with like-minded people is important for your business and your overall well-being in my opinion. I learned this the hard way also. Some people in your life are toxic. Even if they are your best friends or those you love, sometimes it's just better to move on with your life and leave them in the past. I've done it with more than a few people—friends and family.

It was difficult, but I couldn't grow as a person, father, husband, or business professional until I removed all that negativity from my life and focused on the positive. I started to surround myself with people like Patrick Connell, Luis Garibay, Jennifer Walters, Khrystiana Valadez, Fallynn White, my son and my four daughters, and other close family members. Like my wife, they only want to see me succeed and are happy to see me make progress. I had to cut off close family and friends who clearly didn't have my best interests at heart or have my back as I had theirs.

It's not an easy thing to do but is essential for growth. Negativity is distracting, and you don't need that when you're trying to grow your business. I surround myself with trustworthy people who want the same things I want. Some are there just as friends and others with or for me.

DELEGATE, DELEGATE, DELEGATE

Once I was aligned with the right people, my business grew quickly to the point I almost couldn't keep up. The biggest obstacle in my way was me because I refused to delegate tasks. I had employees but was so afraid they wouldn't take care of my clients like I do that I never gave them important tasks. I needed them side by side with me helping clients, but I did not yet have that sort of trust.

You must delegate tasks to your employees or you will burn out eventually like I did. At some point, the work becomes too much and you will get tired, your body will tell you it is done. I worked 20 hours a day for years building my companies. Patrick, my wife, my kids, my nieces, and more told me to slow down or I was going to kill myself. I focused so much on my business that I gained 60 pounds, lost time with my loved ones, worked myself to the bones, and it almost cost me my life.

In 2020, I started having terrible acid reflux because of my weight gain and my lifestyle. I already told you about the health challenges I faced during the past two years, multiple surgeries, COVID-19, sepsis, back-to-back emergency laparotomies two days apart. Fearing the worst, I spoke to my doctor.

"Give it to me straight, Doc," I said to him. "What are my chances."

I could sense his hesitation. "Each patient is different—"

"I can handle the truth. Just tell me like it is."

"At best, most cases like yours have a ten to fifteen percent chance of survival."

I don't wish a moment like this on anyone. What hurts me worse was watching my wife cry in that hospital room when she thought I wasn't looking. Fearing I would die soon, I used the energy I had left to call my CPA, lawyer, and business partner to get things ready for my family.

I will never forget the look on my wife's face when I was making those calls, knowing my kids were at home wondering where Daddy was. My oldest daughters, Jailen and Adyson, were upset. Jailen, sensing that something was very wrong, planned to leave the house to find me, in defiance of her grandparents and my niece who were caring for them.

All that hurt so bad, and why? I chose to eat up the stress until it crushed me like a rock. You're probably wondering why I went so far into detail about this. Because this happens to many people who have done what I did. I don't want this to be you. Maybe it won't be as bad as me, but it can certainly happen.

With my wife's help of and my desire to see my kids again, I made it through.

Once your business is up and running, use your resources. Do your job, and let others do theirs. You will be successful, happier, and have a better work-life balance.

If your current employees cannot complete certain specialized tasks, such as setting up your LLC, payroll, taxes, etc., then look outside your business for help. Have a tax attorney review your returns to make sure everything is one hundred percent on the up and up to avoid issues with the IRS. The cost of my CPA is pennies compared to the savings I realize from using them.

CREATING CONTENT

Now, let's talk more about content creation. Knowing your audience and proper targeting is important, but you must also be able to create content (graphics, videos, etc.) that matches your target demographic . For example, the Austin, Texas population is very music and art-focused, so when I do photo ads for this area, I use artistic and music-style graphics, loud colors, familiar landmarks, etc. In other areas where it may be more business professional, like Dallas, I use clean, red, blue, etc., banners on my graphics. The main point is to know your market and customize your content to speak to them directly. If you can't get their attention with your ad, you fail. I can help with this in my training, so just reach out if you have questions.

SOCIAL MEDIA

You should be continuously active on social media. Create Facebook business page(s), business Instagram, Twitter, YouTube, or whatever you prefer. Get on it, and stay active. Post relevant and helpful content and keep yourself at the top of your audience's mind. "Out of sight, out of mind" is a true statement. If people don't see you frequently, they will forget about you. Look at Coca Cola, for example, they are huge and still advertise. Why? Because they want to remain number one. You must always know your brand. Keep it consistent. Make sure it matches what you do, and continually advertise it. Always keep your brand active to your target audience and current and past clients. My point is, be present and stay present with your target audience. Don't get in front of them and then lose them. Have a plan to keep them.

Make sure you are listening to the market and giving your audience what they want. My clients want help with social media and lead generation. So, the free content I put out is focused on that alone. For agents, their clients want to see homes or sell a home, so they want to advertise listings in the potential client's area or home prices so sellers can see what their home may be worth.

BE YOURSELF

Finally, and most importantly, BE YOURSELF! Work with clients that understand you and can relate to you, and whom you can relate to as well. Don't just surround yourself with like-minded people; work with them. I see so many people trying to fake their way through a client meeting, acting like someone they think the client wants. Eventually, they will see you for who you are. Whether that is good or bad doesn't matter because they will know you aren't who they thought you were. Just be yourself, and you will find clients who think you are great for the job just the way you are. They will refer others to you, and your business will grow.

I will give you three examples. I have tattoos. I only wear sweats, Nike shorts, t-shirts, and Air Max shoes. I do not dress up for meetings. Don't get me wrong; I am not against suits. I just like being myself. I do not wear suits to meet clients and do not pretend to be somebody else. I have sold (dozens, hundreds, thousands?) of houses and trained more than 48,000 agents in ten countries to date. I did that by being myself.

I highly respect two other very successful people in the industry. First is Nathan Carroll, for whom I have a great amount of respect. He is who he is and doesn't change for anyone. The dude lives his life. He works with like-minded people. He acts like who he is, and he owns that shit.

He has built a nice following in the industry and does a ton of business. He has probably sold more houses than you! (If you look him up, you'll understand what I said that.)

Second is Justin Mercer, The Tattooed REALTOR. Honestly, I have yet to see someone besides myself build their business so fast by owning who they are. He is the perfect example of what I mean when I say, "Be yourself and own that shit." The dude has tattoos all over his body (I am headed that way too) and has built his brand around it. Now he is not only selling millions of dollars of real estate each year, but he's also doing speaking engagements and training. He broke the mold and showed this industry that you don't have to do shit you don't want to do. You can be you and kill it! He did what I did, just in a different market, with a slightly different product. He works with clients to buy and sell real estate. I train agents on how to generate leads for their businesses.

Justin and Nathan are perfect examples of being yourself and working with only like-minded people in the real estate industry. Nathan, Justin, and I have probably been rejected by potential clients more times than we can count, but that shit doesn't matter. Why? Because for every client that rejected us, we picked up five more who did. That, my friends, is how you win.

I have worked hard all my life to get to where I am today; nothing was handed to me, I worked myself almost to death, and I am still growing and learning from people I respect, and from you all. I learn something new from my clients every day.

From the moment I wake up, I remember where I came from, the streets of Galveston, running from the police, selling drugs, doing bad things to try and survive to get where I am now. It was hard. It was painful at times. It was scary. It was lonely. But it is possible to change your circumstances and become something more, something great.

My experiences made me the man I am today. I hope you take to heart everything I have shared with you in this book— the good, the bad, the ugly—and use it wisely in your struggle to success. Just like I did.

ACKNOWLEDGMENTS

I hesitated to include this because I have so many people to thank and do not want to miss anyone. So many helped me on my journey for the last ten years, sticking by my side, helping me grow our businesses, and supporting me when others thought I would fail.

But when it comes to inspiration for this book, my grandmother Mary Christine Hegmann comes first. She always told me I could grow up to do amazing things. She was one of the only supportive people in my life, even after I lost my way. And after she died, I always came back to her encouraging words. "You can do anything you want, and don't let anyone tell you otherwise." With the mindset she gave me, I always wanted to make her proud of my accomplishments. I hope that wherever she is, she can see what I have done during the past decade and read how much she inspired me in my book. Nanny, I love and miss you so much.

I am thankful for my sister Lilia Christine Scallon, who was more like a mother to me when I was growing up. Even though we lived some distance apart, we talked frequently, and I looked up to her like few others. I am grateful that she encouraged me to move to Austin from Galveston, which turned out to be the right path for changing my life. I love you.

To Patrick Connell, my business partner, best friend, brother, your support and friendship have helped me grow as a person and business professional in ways I never imagined. I am sure we have both taught each other many valuable lessons. The companies we have built together and our team are nothing short of amazing to me. Thank you for everything, for being there for me at my lowest points and carrying all of that weight on your back without me for a while.

To my team, Jen Walters, Khrystiana Valadez, Glenna Machado, and Lorene Connell, among many others. Thank you for your dedication and hard work, and for supporting Patrick and me through thick and thin. All of you are amazing souls, and I am honored to have had you by my side throughout most of this journey. You all are more than just employees. You are family, and we appreciate everything that you do.

To Dunbar Campbell, I am not even sure what to say, but I'll take a crack at it. You took my life story and helped me write the first half of this book when I couldn't. It was hard for me to write the words myself without emotion standing in my way. You took my story and translated it amazingly well. You have been a great friend and mentor to me throughout this process, and I owe you a lot for that.

To Allen Harris, when I first met you at Dell Waco in 2003, I was rough around the edges. I was still in my survival mode at only 18 years old, with no idea how to sell anything or talk to clients on the phone. Your guidance, management skills, friendship, and understanding helped make me the business professional I am today. You could have fired me more than a few times for things I screwed up, but I think you saw in me what I didn't see in myself. I know we don't see each other or talk very often, but I want you to know your impact on my life and how much I look up to you. Thank you for your friendship and mentorship.

To Tim Cline, you, my friend, may not have known how much of a difference you made in my life. We met at Dell Waco when I moved from Allen's team to yours in 2004. I was a little better than in 2003, but you helped push me to new heights. You taught me how to sell and conduct myself in the office, and you were more like a friend than a manager. Tough at times, but always from a good place to teach us how to grow. I am grateful for all that I learned from you, inside and outside of that office. Thank you for being a great friend and manager.

To Andre Artis, this will be a long one, but I will try to keep it short. On New Year's Eve, 2005, you called me after you and Lori Nunez interviewed me a few days prior for a position in the Dell Business Department in Round Rock. I believe you said, "Are you ready to come to Round Rock and be on my team?" This call and an opportunity changed my life. Although the dice rolled differently, and I ended up on someone else's team, you gave me that shot. Throughout my time there, we were still in the same area, and I learned a ton from you. I watched how you did business in the office and how you created ventures outside of the office. You lit the entrepreneurial fire under me, from how you started your club in Killeen to the multiple Krab Kingz restaurants and other ventures. I have watched your successes from afar and tried to model myself after you. You are a great mentor, businessman, and a great father. All things I respect tremendously. Thank you for all that you do.

To my in-laws, well, I should say Mom and Dad, I knew I was in the right place from the day I met you guys. You have trusted me, loved me, and treated me like one of your own for almost half of my life. Thank you for all that you do for us and the rest of our amazing family. We love you very much.

To my children, without the five of you, I doubt I could do any of the things I do daily. Everything I do is for you. You are the reason I wake up in the morning. Sometimes, when I take a trip for a few days to get away by myself, I am ready to get back to you even before I fall asleep on the first night. The love I have for you is out of this world. I love you all and can't wait to look back on your lives ten years from now to see how far you have come.

To the rest of my family, thank you for being there for me, Leticia, and the kids. We all help each other in many ways, but many of you stepped up and took control when I got sick in 2020 and 2021. It was amazing to see how much you all cared, and it further reinforced what I already knew. We have a bond that can't be broken. You would do anything for us, and we would do anything for you. All of you have inspired me to continue to grow in many ways in life, and for that and your love, I thank you.

Finally, and most importantly, to my amazing wife. I don't even know where to start. I have loved you since the first day we met in 2004. Not long after that, I knew we were meant to be together. I was in love at 19 years old, and I have been (for the first time in my life) happy every day since. You have been there with and for me from day one when we didn't have a dime. You have loved me, supported all my insane dreams, and helped me grow our family and businesses to where we are today. You took care of me at my lowest points in life, literally nursed me back to health when I was almost gone, and never once wavered or gave it a second thought. I would do anything for you, literally ANYTHING. Without you, there is no me, and I would be lost. I, and all the people I have around me that I have been able to help, owe it all to you. You are the core of everything I do and the reason I keep doing it. I love you and look forward to seeing what comes next for us.

IN REMEMBRANCE

We extend our deepest condolences to the family and friends of Evelyn Kusch, CEO of White Bird Publications. She helped hundreds of writers fulfill their dream of writing and publishing their stories. Since she left us before "The Struggle to Success" could become a reality, another publisher has stepped up to get us to print. May she rest in peace.

ABOUT WILLIAM HEGMANN

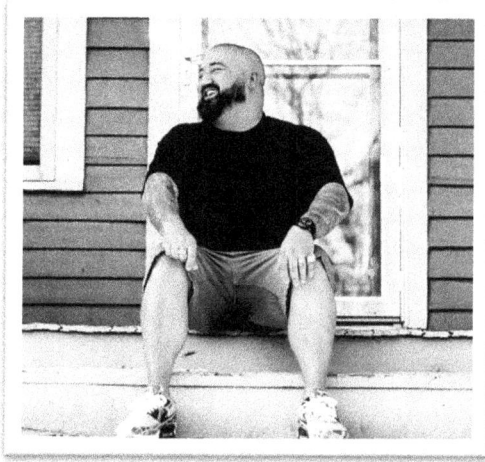

William Hegmann wrote his life story so other people, especially youth, would be inspired to change their lives for the better. Born and raised in Galveston, he dropped out of school and joined the crime-infested streets of the city. As a troubled teenager roaming dangerous neighborhoods, he was well on his way to becoming a tragic statistic like many people he knew. Some died violently, several from drug overdoses, and others landed in prison.

William was not supposed to make it to twenty.

But a close call with death gave him reason to change his life. Staring up at the ceiling from a hospital bed, he decided to change his path.

He recognized that education was his pathway off the streets. He entered Job Corps, earned his GED, then went to Texas State Technical College to learn web software and design and computer programming, skills that would be valuable in his later businesses. Using his education and desire for real achievement, he talked his way into a marketing position for Dell Computers. For nine consecutive quarters, he was the Representative of the Quarter. He was on his way.

ACKNOWLEDGMENTS

With growing confidence that hard work, the willingness to learn, and the right mentors around him, he could be a successful entrepreneur. William started several businesses while still employed at Dell. He eventually left Dell and developed his most successful business, The Social Agent. This book, "The Struggle to Success," takes readers in William's footsteps from the streets of Galveston to the luxuries and freedom of financial success with the lessons everyone needs to learn to achieve more in life.

MORE INFORMATION

Are you interested in mentoring or coaching for yourself or your team to help scale your business faster? If so, contact me through any of the outlets below!

Text Me
512-915-3400

Email
william@williamhegmann.com

Join Tens of Thousands of Others in our Facebook Group
https://www.facebook.com/groups/thesocialagentusa

The Social Agent University
www.socialagentuniversity.com

Real Estate Brokerage
www.realtysolutionsteam.com

Home Renovations, Remodeling and Roofing Services
www.dashconstructiontx.com

CRM link
www.SocialCRMPro.com

Home Offers Made Easy
www.HomeOffersMadeEasy.com

My Website
www.WilliamHegmann.com

Subscribe to Our Business YouTube for a Wealth of Content!
https://www.youtube.com/user/williamhegmann

www.ingramcontent.com/pod-product-compliance
Lightning Source LLC
Chambersburg PA
CBHW060039210326
41520CB00009B/1185